Telecourse Guide
for

AMERICA
IN PERSPECTIVE

U.S. History Since 1877

Telecourse Guide
for

A MERICA
IN PERSPECTIVE
U.S. History Since 1877

Fourth Edition

Kenneth G. Alfers, Ph.D.

Produced by:

DALLAS TeleLearning
Dallas County Community College District

Addison Wesley Longman
America in Perspective is produced by the Dallas County Community College District, R. Jan LeCroy Center for Educational Telecommunications in association with the Higher Education Telecommunications Association of Oklahoma, Texas Consortium for Educational Telecommunications, Northern Illinois Learning Resources Cooperative, State of Florida Department of Education, and Amarillo College, and in cooperation with Addison Wesley Longman Publishers.

ISBN:0-321-08451-9
Copyright © 2001 by Dallas County Community College District.

DALLAS TeleLearning
9596 Walnut Street
Dallas, Texas 75243

This edition has been printed directly from camera-ready copy. Photographs reproduced herein were supplied by the Dallas County Community College District archives.

Printed in the United States of America
10 9 8 7 6 5 4 3 2 1

Dedication

To Molly, Andrew, and Michael
and
To all students of history

Acknowledgments

Special thanks are due to some special people who greatly enhanced the quality of this course. Nora Busby, Instructional Designer, constantly kept the focus of my work on student learning. Her commitment to quality is unquestioned and unrelenting, and she has my utmost respect. The work of Phil Johnson, Producer/Director, is most obvious in the twenty-six video programs, which demonstrate his brilliance and insight. Dr. Bill Mugleston, my colleague for over fifteen years, served as a Research Associate on this project. In addition to uncovering documentary and visual sources, his thoughtful comments always improved the final product.

David Molina, Associate Producer, and Darise Error, Production Assistant, were always available with whatever logistical support I needed. Paul Bosner, Project Manager, gave us all the benefit of his experience and encouragement. My colleagues on the national and local advisory committees deserve recognition for their constructive comments throughout the entire process.

In addition to those mentioned above, I would like to thank Pamela K. Quinn, Dorothy J. Clark, Bob Crook, Ted Pohrte, Bob Peterson, Terry Error, Mary Bills, Janet Fulton, Steven Richards, Jacquelyn Tulloch, Betsy Turner, Evelyn Wong, and all other members of the staff of the R. Jan LeCroy Center for Educational Telecommunications for making my work with the Center so pleasant and rewarding. Although not directly associated with the LeCroy Center, Margot Olson, a Test Design Specialist, helped clarify hundreds of items in the test bank.

For the fourth edition of this telecourse guide, I have had the special assistance of Dr. Carole N. Lester. She has updated the telecourse guide to assure proper coordination with the latest edition of the textbook.

—Kenneth G. Alfers
History Content Specialist

Contents

To the Student

How often do you hear that something "needs to be put in perspective"? In other words, we are constantly seeking a meaningful relationship among all the facts and happenings to which we are constantly exposed in our information age. This is essentially what I and the others involved in the production have endeavored to do in this telecourse, *America in Perspective*. We want you to reach a better understanding of how and why the United States came to be what it is today. In the process of accomplishing that goal, we have produced a comprehensive course of study that challenges you to think. We have tried to help you develop an analytical frame of reference which you can use to make sense of the past as well as the present.

I have been teaching American history at the college level for over twenty-five years. During the 1990-91 and 1991-92 academic years, I concentrated totally on preparing materials for this telecourse. Friends, colleagues, and former students sometimes smile and wonder why I devoted so much time to the creation of a new history course. After all, what changes in history? Indeed, that is a great part of my fascination with the discipline, for there is always more to learn. For example, I hope you will be as intrigued as I was by the remarks of the forty-one nationally recognized scholars whom we interviewed for *America in Perspective*. Their insights make this course truly unique.

America in Perspective surveys United States history since 1877 in twenty-six lessons. In each lesson, we try to connect you with ordinary people who lived in earlier times. In addition, each video program uses location footage to remind us that we all encounter the past in our daily lives and in our contemporary communities.

In summary, I want you to think about the American people, past and present, and to consider the relationship of the United States with the rest of the world. Our personal lives, our nation, and our world demand that we analyze, evaluate, and make reasoned judgments about people, leaders, positions, and issues. Our future depends on the prudent application of our knowledge. Through this course of study, it is my hope and expectation that all of us can more thoughtfully put America in perspective.

—Kenneth G. Alfers

About the Author

Dr. Kenneth G. Alfers is a teacher, writer, and historian. He received the Dallas County Community College District's Outstanding Teacher Award in 1983. He was the Content Specialist for *America: The Second Century,* an award-winning telecourse used around the country since 1980. He received his B.A. and M.A. degrees from Creighton University and his M.Ph. and Ph.D. degrees from The George Washington University.

A Final Note

With careful and thoughtful application of your time and energy to the material presented in this course, you should have a rewarding experience in the broadest sense of that term. I, along with other members of the production team, have put forth our best efforts to create a quality course. However, my experience teaches me that any course can be improved, so I encourage you to share any ideas about it with me. Please send your comments to Kenneth G. Alfers, R. Jan LeCroy Center for Educational Telecommunications, 9596 Walnut Street, Dallas, TX 75243-2112.

Telecourse Organization

America in Perspective is designed as a comprehensive learning package consisting of three elements: telecourse guide, textbooks, and video programs.

TELECOURSE GUIDE

The telecourse guide for this course is:

Alfers, Kenneth. *Telecourse Guide for America in Perspective*, 4th ed. New York: Addison Wesley Longman, 2001.

The telecourse guide acts as your daily instructor. If you follow the Study Guidelines carefully, you should successfully accomplish all the requirements for this course. (See the section entitled "Study Guidelines.")

TEXTBOOKS

In addition to the telecourse guide, there are two books required for this course:

Text: Nash, Gary B., Julie Roy Jeffrey, et al. *The American People: Creating a Nation and a Society, Volume II: From 1865*, 5th ed. New York, Addison Wesley Longman, 2001.

As the title suggests, this text emphasizes the people who have created the nation and the society in which we live. In addition, the authors incorporate the latest scholarship and provide fresh interpretations of the American past.

Reader: Alfers, Kenneth G., C. Larry Pool, and William Mugleston, *Perspectives on America, Volume 2: Readings in United States History From 1877*. New York: Forbes Custom Publishing, 1997.

This collection of articles provides opportunities to explore specific topics in more depth.

The specific reading assignment appears at the beginning of each lesson in the telecourse guide. Be sure to read this material before viewing the video program.

VIDEO PROGRAMS

The video program series for this telecourse is:

America in Perspective.

Each video program is correlated with the telecourse guide and the lesson assignment for that lesson. Be sure to read the Video Focus Points in the telecourse guide before you watch the program. The video programs are presented in a documentary format and are designed to bring analysis and perspective to the issues being discussed. Watch them closely.

If the programs are broadcast more than once in your area, or if video or audio tapes are available at your college, you might find it helpful to watch the video programs more than once or to listen to an audio tape for review. Since examination questions will be taken from the video programs as well as from the readings, careful attention to both is vital to your success.

TELECOURSE PLUS

An online interactive option is available to students whose institutions have opted to license it. The web activities are useful for working with "real-time" information related to the lesson content and objectives. If your course includes this PLUS component, please consult your instructor for the course website address and required password.

Study Guidelines

Follow these guidelines as you study the material presented in each lesson:

1. **LESSON ASSIGNMENT—**
   Review the Lesson Assignment in order to schedule your time appropriately. Pay careful attention; the titles and numbers of the textbook chapter, the telecourse guide lesson, and the video program may be different from one another.

2. **OVERVIEW—**
   Read the Overview for an introduction to the lesson material.

3. **LEARNING OBJECTIVES—**
   Review the Learning Objectives and pay particular attention to the lesson material that relates to them.

4. **TEXT FOCUS POINTS—**
   To get the most from your reading, review the Text Focus Points, then read the assignment. You may want to write responses or notes to reinforce what you have learned.

5. **READER FOCUS POINTS—**
   To get the most from your reading, review the Reader Focus Points, then read the assignment. After completing the assignment, write responses and/or notes to reinforce what you have learned.

6. **VIDEO FOCUS POINTS—**
   To get the most from the video segment of the lesson, review the Video Focus Points, then watch the video. You may want to write responses or notes to reinforce what you have learned.

7. **ENRICHMENT IDEAS—**
   The Enrichment Ideas are not required unless your instructor assigns them. They are offered as suggestions to help you learn more about the material presented in this lesson.

8. SUGGESTED READINGS—
    The Suggested Readings are designed to encourage you to go beyond the elements required in the course.

9. SUGGESTED WEB SITES—
    Several places in the textbook will include information marked "The History Place." These are references to related web sites. See the "Suggested Web Sites" at the end of the chapters of the textbook if you wish to further explore the material presented in this lesson.

10. PRACTICE TEST—
    The items in the practice test will help you evaluate your understanding of this lesson. Use the answer key at the end of the lesson to check your answers or to locate material related in each question.

11. ANSWER KEY
    The answer key provides answers and references for the Practice Test questions. Focus Points are referenced using the following abbreviations: $T = $ Text, $V = $ Video, and $R = $ Reader.

Unit One:
An Industrializing People
1877-1900

1. The Closing of the Frontier

2. The Rise of Big Business

3. Labor's Struggle

4. The Huddled Masses

5. The American Dream Deferred

6. The Populist Challenge

7. War and Empire

By 1877, the turmoil of the Civil War and Reconstruction was over for most Americans. People now became more absorbed in the ongoing transformation of the United States into an industrial nation. The process of closing the last frontier satisfied neither the American Indians nor the settlers who took their place. Meanwhile, industrialization, urbanization, and immigration changed America forever. People shared the joys of daily life and coped with their hardships. Minorities, particularly American Indians and African Americans, seemed almost helpless as their dreams were deferred. Those better able to protest against their plight, laborers and farmers, organized to challenge the power of the political and economic establishment. Meanwhile, by the late 1890s, the industrial nation stretched its influence into the international arena as never before. The nation and the world would never again be the same.

Lesson 1

The Closing of the Frontier

LESSON ASSIGNMENTS

Review the following assignments in order to schedule your time appropriately. Pay careful attention; the titles and numbers of the textbook chapter, the telecourse guide lesson, and the video program may be different from one another.

Text: Nash et al., *The American People, Volume Two: From 1865*, Chapter 17, "The Realities of Rural America," pp. 528-560.

Video: "The Closing of the Frontier," from the series *America in Perspective*.

OVERVIEW

In this lesson we want to examine the myths and the realities of the non-Indian settlement of the "last frontier." Most of the non-Indians who moved into the Great Plains area in the late nineteenth century had visions of adventure, opportunity, and perhaps even wealth. For many, the realities of life on the plains were quite disillusioning. Meanwhile, the Plains Indians viewed this frontier settlement from a vastly different perspective. Their way of life was being threatened, and many of their hopes and dreams were being shattered. In some ways this clash of cultures, which had gone on for centuries, was coming to an end that left both groups dissatisfied and desperate.

At the close of the Civil War, there still existed a vast reservoir of land untapped by non-Indian settlers. The expanse of plains, mountains, and desert between the Missouri River and California lay ready for development. Within a single generation, almost all the land was occupied. The United States Census Report of 1890 summed up a significant turning point in American history when it stated that "the unsettled area had been so broken into by isolated bodies of settlement that there can hardly be said to be a frontier line."

Miners and range cattle ranchers generally preceded farmers into the "last frontier," but the farmers became more permanent settlers. Lured by a generous federal land policy and enticing railroad promotions, farmers moved into an area previously thought not to be conducive to agriculture. They hoped that use of new technology, such as windmills, steel plows, barbed wire, and ultimately all sorts of farm machinery, would help them perpetuate the "myth of the happy yeoman." This concept held that the farmer, or yeoman, was an exceptional human being. Working close to nature, the farmer had a special calling and was the center of all enterprise. The farmer was thought to be hard working, dependable, scrupulously honest, and satisfied with life. Life on the plains, and the fact that farming in general was becoming more of a business, challenged the "happy yeoman" ideal.

Meanwhile, the American Indians who lived in the area being "settled" by non-Indians tried to maintain their territory and their identity. Long unfairly stereotyped as "merciless Indian savages" by those desiring their land, their choices were the same as they had been for centuries: resistance or accommodation. Even though Indian resistance was doomed to fail, we can understand why some Indians made that choice. By 1890 the era of Indian "wars" was over. Years earlier, in 1877, Chief Joseph of the Nez Percé had given eloquent expression to the plight of the Indians in the late nineteenth century: "Hear me my Chiefs, I am tired; my heart is sick and sad. From where the sun now stands, I will fight no more forever."

So, by the 1890s the centuries-long process of settling the frontier had come to an end. Life on the agricultural frontier was difficult, yet some survived and established homesteads which were passed down for generations. Others, who had looked to the frontier for freedom and opportunities, began to look elsewhere. As farming became more of a business, the ideal of the "happy yeoman" became even harder to achieve. American Indians could find little consolation, for their situation seemed almost totally depressing. Their lives would never be the same, and they and the rest of society have been adjusting ever since. For many farmers and most Indians, the future looked bleak in 1890. America was well on its way to becoming a nation of factories and cities

LEARNING OBJECTIVES

Goal—The purpose of "The Closing of the Frontier" is to increase our understanding of the reasons for the settlement of the last frontier and the realities of life on the frontier for both the non-Indian settlers and the American Indians already in the area.

Objectives—Upon completing this lesson, you should be able to:
1. Describe the myth and reality regarding farming in the late nineteenth century.
2. Describe and explain the reasons for the relatively rapid settlement of the Great Plains between 1865 and 1890.
3. Discuss the characteristics of cattle ranching.
4. Examine the realities of life on the California frontier.
5. Examine the results of the cultural and military conflict between American Indians and non-Indians during the late nineteenth century.

TEXT FOCUS POINTS

The following questions are designed to help you get the most from your reading. Review them before you do your reading. After completing the assignment, write responses and/or notes to reinforce what you have learned.

Text: Nash et al., *The American People,* Chapter 17, pp. 528-560.

1. What was the "rural myth"? Describe the reality of farming.
2. How and why did farming become a business in the late nineteenth century?
3. How did falling prices for farm products affect farming operations?
4. What factors encouraged farmers to settle the plains in the late nineteenth century? Which immigrant groups were most likely to settle on the plains? What was life like on the plains?
5. What factors explain the rise of the cattle frontier? How and why did cattle ranchers have to adjust by the late nineteenth century?
6. How and why was California farming different from that going on in most of the rest of the country? How did the farming, ranching, and mining in the West affect the nation's natural resources?
7. What was "the white perspective" regarding the Plains Indians?
8. In general, what was the Indian's view of the incursion by non-Indians onto their lands? How did they react?
9. Why was the Dawes Act passed? What were the effects of the act?

10. What explains the popularity of "ghost dancing"? What resulted from it?

VIDEO FOCUS POINTS

The following questions are designed to help you get the most from the video segment of this lesson. Review them before you watch the video. After viewing the video segment, write responses and/or notes to reinforce what you have learned.

Video: "The Closing of the Frontier"

1. What factors contributed to non-Indian settlement of the last frontier?
2. From the perspective of the American Indians, what choices did they have regarding non-Indian settlement? What resulted from the clash of cultures taking place in the late nineteenth century?
3. Describe the conditions for the non-Indian men and women who settled the plains. How did they cope with the realities of their situations?
4. What was the status of the Plains Indians by 1890?
5. How real was the myth of the happy yeoman by 1890? How and why was the myth modified in the twentieth century?

ENRICHMENT IDEAS

These activities are not required unless your instructor assigns them. They are offered as suggestions to help you learn more about the material presented in this lesson.

1. Read and analyze the "Recovering the Past" section of *The American People* text on pages 544-545. Write a 750-word essay in which you deal with the questions in the text. How did the magazines of the day provide insight on the events of the time and help shape the perspectives and values of late-nineteenth-century men and women?
2. You are a man or a woman settler on the Great Plains in the early 1880s. Write a 750-word letter to a relative living on the East Coast in which you describe your life on the frontier.
3. You are a chief of an Indian tribe living on the Great Plains in the late 1870s. Prepare a 750-word speech to be delivered to the tribal council in which you

recommend what your tribe should do in light of white settlers' incursion onto tribal lands.

4. Read the article entitled "Last Ghastly Moments at the Little Bighorn," in *Perspectives on America*. Then write a 750-word essay in which you analyze the factors which led to the battle and the reasons for Indian victory.

SUGGESTED READINGS

See the "Recommended Reading" listings on page 559 of the textbook if you wish to explore further the material presented in this lesson.

SUGGESTED WEB SITES

Several places in the textbook will include information marked "The History Place." This is a reference to a related web site. See the "Suggested Web Sites" at the end of the chapter of the textbook if you wish to further explore the material presented in this lesson.

PRACTICE TEST

The following items will help you evaluate your understanding of this lesson. Use the answer key at the end of the lesson to check your answers or to locate material related in each question.

MULTIPLE-CHOICE INSTRUCTIONS

Choose the single best answer. If more than one answer is required, it will be so indicated.

1. The "rural myth" or the "myth of the happy yeoman" conveyed all of the following ideas EXCEPT that farmers were
   A. sturdy and individualistic.
   B. happy and healthy.
   C. satisfied and secure.
   D. wealthy and powerful.

2. An important factor in transforming the nature of American agriculture after the Civil War was the
   A. decline in international markets for American farm products.
   B. increasing utilization of machinery.
   C. scarcity of land in the Great Plains.
   D. decrease in the size of the average farm.

3. One result of falling prices for agricultural products in the late nineteenth century was
   A. pressure to produce more.
   B. relief of the debt burden for farmers.
   C. less acreage under cultivation.
   D. reduction of the real value of farm debts.

4. An important factor in promoting settlement of the Great Plains was
   A. the construction of railroads in that region.
   B. the decline in farm indebtedness.
   C. inflationary economic conditions.
   D. the elimination of Indian resistance to white settlement by 1876.

5. By the mid-1880s, cattleraising in the American West
   A. remained highly successful using open-range techniques.
   B. faced numerous problems from both people and nature.
   C. prevented settlement of the area by farmers.
   D. proved highly profitable for the legendary cowboys.

6. The development of agriculture in California during the late nineteenth century was characterized by
   A. small family farms.
   B. large profits for original Mexican landholders.
   C. production of cotton.
   D. large-scale farming.

7. In the late nineteenth century, whites generally believed that American Indians on the Great Plains should be
   A. recognized for their cultural contributions.
   B. removed from the area through force and/or extermination.
   C. returned to their lands in the East.
   D. given title to their land because they were American citizens.

8. In the last three decades of the nineteenth century, American Indians on the Great Plains
   A. accepted their removal to reservations without resistance.
   B. generally believed that government had treated them fairly.
   C. eagerly adopted sedentary ways of the whites.
   D. often fiercely resisted white settlement.

9. The primary effect of the Dawes Act was that American Indians
   A. gained respect for their tribal identity.
   B. acquired better living conditions on their reservations.
   C. retained mineral rights even when their land was sold.
   D. lost title to vast amounts of their land.

10. One result of ghost dancing by the American Indians was that
    A. respect for their religious beliefs began to grow.
    B. violence on the Great Plains virtually ended.
    C. whites became uneasy and demanded more protection.
    D. conditions improved on most reservations.

11. A key to survival for settlers on the Great Plains was
    A. making treaties with Indians.
    B. engaging in political activism.
    C. adapting to harsh conditions.
    D. building secure log cabins.

12. In the video program, Professor Gary Anderson described the condition of the Plains Indians by 1890 as being
    A. dismal and depressing.
    B. encouraging and optimistic.
    C. secure and wealthy.
    D. hostile and aggressive.

13. By 1890, the idealized, happy yeoman farmers were
    A. dependent on outside forces.
    B. typical of most settlers on the Great Plains.
    C. still mostly self-sufficient.
    D. anxiously ready to settle the next frontier.

ESSAY/PROBLEM QUESTIONS

14. Describe and explain the development of the myths of the "happy yeoman" and the "merciless Indian savage." How and why did the realities of life for farmers and Indians in the late nineteenth century run counter to the myths?

15. Contrast the white perspective toward the Indians living on the Great Plains during the late nineteenth century with the Indians' view of white settlement in that area during the same time period. In what ways were the actions taken by both groups based on these perspectives?

ANSWER KEY

Answers	Learning Objectives	Focus Points	References
1. D	1	T1	Nash, pp. 530-531
2. B	1	T2	Nash, p. 531
3. A	1	T3	Nash, p. 532
4. A	2	T4, V1	Nash, p. 533, Video
5. B	3	T5	Nash, pp. 537-538
6. D	4	T6	Nash, pp. 538-539
7. B	5	T7	Nash, pp. 541-542
8. D	5	T8, V2	Nash, pp. 542-543, Video
9. D	5	T9, V2	Nash, pp. 543, 546, Video
10. C	5	T10	Nash, pp. 546-547
11. C	1	V3	Video
12. A	5	V4	Video
13. A	1	V5	Video
14.	All	All	Text and Video
15.	All	All	Text and Video

Lesson 2

The Rise of Big Business

LESSON ASSIGNMENTS

Review the following assignments in order to schedule your time appropriately. Pay careful attention; the titles and numbers of the textbook chapter, the telecourse guide lesson, and the video program may be different from one another.

Text: Nash et al., *The American People, Volume Two: From 1865,*
           Chapter 18, "The Rise of Smokestack America," pp. 562-569, 576-582;
           and Chapter 19, "Politics and Reform," pp. 609-611.

Reader: *Perspectives on America, Volume 2,*
           "Epitaph for the Steel Master," by Robert L. Heilbroner.

Video: "The Rise of Big Business,"
           from the series *America in Perspective.*

OVERVIEW

In the late nineteenth century, many factors converged to help transform the United States from a predominantly agricultural to an industrial nation. American enterprise expanded to unprecedented levels of production. Consumers, enticed by advertising, could now envision possessing items only dreamed of by earlier generations. New heroes emerged, as the "self-made" businessman replaced the happy yeoman as the ideal in American society. How had this happened? What were the costs and benefits of the rise of big business?

    As historian Glenn Porter stated in *The Rise of Big Business, 1860-1910,* "In the decades after the Civil War, when people spoke of big business, they had in mind three kinds of enterprises in particular: railroads, manufacturing corporations, and banks." (Arlington Heights, Ill.: AHM Publishing Company, 1973, p. 7.) The leaders of those businesses—the Vanderbilts, the Carnegies, the Rockefellers, the Morgans, and others—personified the changing nature of the economy and the coming of a new economic order which affected everyone. The nature of work, the environment in which people lived, the consumption of material goods, the very quality of life, changed. To cite Professor Porter once again:

> Much good as well as much that was not good has flowed from our industrial, urban nation. . . . It is clear that the modern corporation lies at the heart of twentieth century American civilization. Until we understand how and why we came to have that particular institution, we cannot fully understand our society or intelligently judge the desirability and the possibility of change. (p. 26)

There are at least seven major reasons for the massive industrialization of the United States between the 1870s and 1900. These are:

1. The availability of abundant quantities of natural resources
2. A sufficient supply of common and skilled labor (The next two lessons will present a detailed look at working and living conditions in this era.)
3. Sufficient capital for investment
4. Technological applications to transfer materials into goods and commodities
5. A market system able to distribute and allow for consumption of the items produced
6. Favorable government policies and attitudes at both the state and national levels
7. Managerial techniques and leaders to coordinate and organize large-scale business operations.

These factors were present singularly or on a small scale before the Civil War, but it was during the late nineteenth century that they converged in such a fashion to transform the United States into an industrial giant.

To those at the top of the new economic and social order, this transformation brought great wealth and power. Their status was supported by literature, philosophy, and even religion. To those who could make it to the emerging middle class, the new industrial order offered the possibility of a more comfortable lifestyle. Unfortunately, most people remained at or near the bottom of the class system, and to those working poor and unemployed, industrialization exposed its harshest realities.

LEARNING OBJECTIVES

Goal—The purpose of "The Rise of Big Business" is to increase our understanding of the reasons for the rapid industrialization of the United States in the late nineteenth century and to assess the initial costs and benefits of that process.

Objectives—Upon completing this lesson, you should be able to:
1. Describe and explain the reasons for large-scale industrialization of the United States in the late nineteenth century.
2. Examine how the business class was supported by the culture of the period.
3. Assess the costs as well as the benefits of the rapid industrialization of the United States.

TEXT FOCUS POINTS

The following questions are designed to help you get the most from your reading. Review them before you do your reading. After completing the assignment, write responses and/or notes to reinforce what you have learned.

Text: Nash et al., *The American People,* Chapter 18, pp. 562-569, 576-582; and Chapter 19, pp. 609-611.

1. Describe the key factors which contributed to economic growth during the latter part of the nineteenth century.
2. Why were capital and investment banking institutions important to industrial growth during the late nineteenth century?
3. How were the railroads pioneers of administrative practices and management techniques for big business?
4. What management and organizational techniques were particularly effective in promoting business expansion? What often resulted from these business practices? Why did many businesses incorporate?
5. What characterized the erratic economic cycles of the late nineteenth century? What were the effects of these cycles? How did industrial growth affect the environment?
6. How did industrialization transform the lives of middle-class men and women?

7. What was the "social ethic" of the late nineteenth century and who benefited from it the most? Describe the importance of Horatio Alger, Jr., in the development of the success myth.

8. What was the primary message of Andrew Carnegie's "The Gospel of Wealth"? How did social Darwinism support the rich and powerful?

READER FOCUS POINTS

Reader: *Perspectives on America, Volume 2*, "Epitaph for the Steel Master," by Heilbroner.

1. What did Andrew Carnegie's family environment emphasize?
2. How was Carnegie able to achieve financial success even before his involvement with the steel industry?
3. What factors explain the expansion of Carnegie's steel empire?
4. What explains the quality and quantity of Andrew Carnegie's philanthropy? Why does the author emerge with a "grudging respect" for Carnegie?

VIDEO FOCUS POINTS

The following questions are designed to help you get the most from the video segment of this lesson. Review them before you watch the video. After viewing the video segment, write responses and/or notes to reinforce what you have learned.

Video: "The Rise of Big Business"

1. How and why did large-scale industrialization take place in America in the late nineteenth century?
2. How did Andrew Carnegie establish dominance in the steel industry?
3. What resulted from the management techniques used by oil tycoon John D. Rockefeller and other industrialists of the era?
4. How did the rags-to-riches idea, the concept of social Darwinism, and belief in the Protestant work ethic support the rich and affect the outlook of the rest of society?
5. What were the costs and benefits of the rise of big business in the late nineteenth century?

ENRICHMENT IDEA

This activity is not required unless your instructor assigns it. It is offered as a suggestion to help you learn more about the material presented in this lesson.

1. In "The Gospel of Wealth," Andrew Carnegie wrote: "The man who dies thus rich dies disgraced." Write a 750-word essay in which you analyze why Carnegie wrote that passage and what he meant by it. Do you agree with him? Why or why not?
2. Read the "Technology Changes the American People" segment about the invention of the flush toilet on pages 578-579 of your textbook. Write a 750-word essay discussing technology and its effects on daily family life.

SUGGESTED READINGS

See the "Recommended Reading" listings on pages 599-600 of the textbook if you wish to further explore the material presented in this lesson.

SUGGESTED WEB SITES

Several places in the textbook will include information marked "The History Place." These are references to related web sites. See the "Suggested Web Sites" at the end of the chapters in the textbook if you wish to further explore the material presented in this lesson.

PRACTICE TEST

The following items will help you evaluate your understanding of this lesson. Use the answer key at the end of the lesson to check your answers or to locate material related in each question.

MULTIPLE-CHOICE INSTRUCTIONS

Choose the single best answer. If more than one answer is required, it will be so indicated.

1. Many factors contributed to the rise of industrial productivity including
    A. a growing use of water power.
    B. a reduction in use of coal.
    C. an increase in number of small businesses.
    D. a shift in production to heavy industry.

2. An important factor in the rapid development of industry in the United States during the last half of the nineteenth century was
    A. increasing competition in the oil business.
    B. availability of capital for investment.
    C. stable economic cycles.
    D. federal regulation of monopolistic business practices.

3. Railroads became pioneers in administrative practices and management techniques in the late nineteenth century because they
    A. operated generally within one state's borders.
    B. promoted vigorous competition with each other.
    C. designed relatively cheap administrative facilities.
    D. emphasized division of responsibility and regular flow of information.

4. By using vertical integration of his steel business, Andrew Carnegie was able to
    A. promote competition.
    B. increase profits.
    C. devote more time to writing books.
    D. control the railroads which supplied raw materials.

5. Unlike pre-Civil War economic downturns, the depressions of the late nineteenth century were characterized by
   A. widespread unemployment.
   B. collapsing land values.
   C. bank failures.
   D. federal government relief programs.

6. During the late nineteenth century, the American middle class generally
   A. enjoyed an improved standard of living.
   B. experienced a decline in its standard of living.
   C. maintained its standard of living with fewer family members employed.
   D. discovered few new products on which to spend increased income.

7. The social ethic which prevailed in late-nineteenth-century America stressed that
   A. family background should determine social rank.
   B. the poor should receive government assistance.
   C. greed had more to do with success than good character.
   D. economic success was available to anyone who worked hard.

8. The theory of social Darwinism promoted the idea that the
   A. problems of poverty could be solved by the government action.
   B. duty of every citizen was to get involved in social work.
   C. maldistribution of wealth in society was justifiable.
   D. competitive spirit was immoral.

9. In Scotland, Andrew Carnegie grew up in a family environment which emphasized
   A. acquisition of great wealth.
   B. conservative politics.
   C. the rights of the working class.
   D. loyalty to one's employer.

10. Andrew Carnegie's early financial success was primarily due to his
   A. shrewd investments.
   B. family inheritance.
   C. publishing activities.
   D. income from foundations.

11. Andrew Carnegie's steel empire expanded for all of the following reasons EXCEPT
   A. talented assistants.
   B. sales and management skills.
   C. growing use of steel.
   D. well-treated and satisfied workers.

12. Andrew Carnegie gave much of his fortune away because of
   A. federal and state income taxes.
   B. belief in the "gospel of wealth."
   C. desire to give workers higher wages.
   D. pressure from his top assistants.

13. One result of the management techniques of John D. Rockefeller and other industrialists of the late nineteenth century was
   A. the use of the business trust to control an industry.
   B. the development of greater competition.
   C. the disappearance of the urban middle class.
   D. a more even distribution of income.

14. One benefit of the rise of big business in the late nineteenth century was
   A. less class structure.
   B. greater protection of workers' rights.
   C. lower cost for producing goods and services.
   D. diminishing corruption in business and politics.

ESSAY/PROBLEM QUESTION

15. Describe and explain at least five major reasons for the rapid industrialization of the United States in the late nineteenth century. How did large-scale industrialization transform life in the United States?

ANSWER KEY

Answers	Learning Objectives	Focus Points	References
1. D	1	T1	Nash, p. 568
2. B	1	T2, V1	Nash, p. 568 and Video
3. D	1	T3	Nash, pp.565-567
4. B	2	T4	Nash, pp. 567-568
5. A	1	T5	Nash, p. 568
6. A	3	T6	Nash, p. 576
7. D	2	T7, V4	Nash, p. 576 and Video
8. C	2	T8, V4	Nash, pp. 610-611 and Video
9. C	1	R1	Reader
10. A	1	R2	Reader
11. D	1	R3, V2	Reader and Video
12. B	3	R4	Reader
13. A	3	V3	Video
14. C	3	V5	Video
15.	All	All	Text, Reader, and Video

Lesson 3

Labor's Struggle

LESSON ASSIGNMENTS

Review the following assignments in order to schedule your time appropriately. Pay careful attention; the titles and numbers of the textbook chapter, the telecourse guide lesson, and the video program may be different from one another.

Text: Nash et al., *The American People, Volume Two: From 1865*, Chapter 18, "The Rise of Smokestack America," pp. 582-600.

Reader: *Perspectives on America, Volume 2*, "The Haymarket: Strike and Violence in Chicago," by R. Jackson Wilson.

Video: "Labor's Struggle," from the series *America in Perspective*.

OVERVIEW

The emergence of big business in the late nineteenth century depended in no small part on the availability of labor. Indeed, workers were plentiful, with millions of immigrants supplementing the indigenous labor force. Mere survival as well as the Horatio Alger dream motivated the workers. In this lesson, we want to examine the realities of life for factory workers. In their attempts to cope with their situation, many workers turned to unionization. In turn, the union movement led to staunch resistance from management, resulting in some of the most violent episodes in labor-management history.

Laborers entered the second century of U.S. history with their attention focused on the great railroad strike of 1877. The strike had been provoked by the series of wage cuts made by many railroad lines as they attempted to maintain profits during the hard times of the mid-1870s. Before the national wave of strikes was crushed by police, troops, and management resistance, scores of people had been killed and injured and property extensively damaged. The work stoppage and the violence associated with it had brought little in the way of financial gains to the workers. Some railroads rescinded their wage cuts, but most brought in strikebreakers or scabs to move the trains once again. The striking workers were often left without jobs, perhaps taking solace in the knowledge that at least they had made a point. "Now managers knew that their men had real grievances that must be listened to. Workers were not dirt or stone, but human beings with dignity and pride." (*Bread and Roses: The Struggle of American Labor 1865-1915*, New York: New American Library, 1977, p. 94.)

Although the standard of living of the laboring class improved somewhat in the decades after the labor disruptions of 1877, the complaints of workers in the age of industrialism were many. While skilled workers might fare fairly well, long hours, low pay, and dangerous working conditions combined to make life especially dreary for unskilled factory workers. Thousands of workers, especially in the iron and steel industry, worked almost seventy hours per week. Women workers, of whom there were thousands, usually received much less than the average pay and worked even more hours. In summary, life for the factory and mine workers during the last quarter of the nineteenth century was generally hard, and their dreams of a real-life Horatio Alger story disintegrated as their bodies weakened with work and age.

As industrialism picked up pace, the industrial workers felt increasingly powerless to deal with the massive impersonal corporations which seemed to control their lives. When they turned to collective action, or unions, management resisted strongly. Managers perceived unions as threats to their power to control the affairs of the corporation.

Unions had existed before the Civil War, but they had been local and regional in scope and organized along craft lines. Post-Civil War unions became national, reflecting what had happened with big business. Regardless of their scope, organizational structure, or philosophy, however, late-nineteenth-century unions were generally battered and busted by the combined strength of business and government. The incidents at Haymarket, Homestead, and Pullman illustrated the hard times for unions and workers. Most could only hope that the new century would provide new opportunities to improve their lot.

Work and the work force today are quite different from what they were a century ago. As we attempt to understand why, we must place the worker/union experience of the late nineteenth century in perspective. That experience can teach us much about how people dealt with the realities of the working conditions of their times and how change comes about in American society.

LEARNING OBJECTIVES

Goal—The purpose of this lesson is to increase our understanding of the realities of life and the reactions of the working class in late-nineteenth-century America.

Objectives—Upon completing this lesson, you should be able to:
1. Describe the composition of the work force, the nature of work, and the working conditions in the late nineteenth century.
2. Analyze the formation, leadership, goals, and relative success of national labor unions during this period.
3. Analyze the resistance to unions by management and government, culminating in large-scale industrial violence.
4. Assess the status of the American worker at the end of the nineteenth century.

TEXT FOCUS POINTS

The following questions are designed to help you get the most from your reading. Review them before you do your reading. After completing the assignment, write responses and/or notes to reinforce what you have learned.

Text: Nash et al., *The American People*, Chapter 18, pp. 582-600.

1. What were the effects of ethnic diversity on the industrial work force?
2. How did industrialization change the nature of work itself?
3. Describe the working conditions for the majority of workers.
4. Which categories of industrial workers benefited most and least from industrialization? Why?
5. How did working-class families cope? Why was child labor common? What role did women play, both inside and outside the family unit?
6. How and why did workers engage in on-the-job protests? Why did strikes become more common after 1876?
7. Describe the significance of the National Labor Union and the Knights of Labor. Why did they generally fail to accomplish their objectives?
8. Describe the significance of the American Federation of Labor. Why was it more successful than other unions? Why was Samuel Gompers important?

9. Describe and explain the strike activity and industrial violence as it affected silver miners and workers at Homestead and Pullman. What is the significance of Eugene V. Debs in the labor movement?
10. In general, why did unions fail in the late nineteenth century?

READER FOCUS POINTS

Reader: *Perspectives on America, Volume 2*, "The Haymarket: Strike and Violence in Chicago," by Wilson.

1. What were the causes and effects of the strike activity at the McCormick company in 1885-1886?
2. Why were workers meeting in Haymarket Square on the night of May 4, 1886? What explains the violence that took place there? What were the immediate effects of that violence?
3. What effect did public attitude have on the trial of the "anarchists"? Why were they found guilty?

VIDEO FOCUS POINTS

The following questions are designed to help you get the most from the video segment of this lesson. Review them before you watch the video. After viewing the video segment, write responses and/or notes to reinforce what you have learned.

Video: "Labor's Struggle"

1. Describe the industrial work force of the late nineteenth century. Why were there so many immigrants and children in the work force?
2. What were the views of management regarding the working conditions, hours, and wages of the laborers?
3. Why did workers organize and engage in strikes? Why did so many strikes result in violence? Why did strikes generally fail?
4. Why was there little public support for unions during this era?
5. What gains had been made by unions and workers by the end of the nineteenth century? What explains their successes and their limitations?

ENRICHMENT IDEAS

These activities are not required unless your instructor assigns them. They are offered as suggestions to help you learn more about the material presented in this lesson.

1. Read and analyze the "Recovering the Past" section of *The American People* text on pages 588-589. Write a 750-word essay in which you deal with the questions in the text. How did ethical beliefs and economic realities separate the social classes? Is this still the case?
2. You are a union organizer in the late nineteenth century trying to persuade workers to join the union. In a 750-word position paper, present your best case for membership.
3. If you are not a union member, interview someone who is, asking him or her to cite his or her reasons for being a union member. Then write a report summarizing your findings and stating your own conclusions about union workers.
4. If you are a union member, interview someone who is not, asking him or her to cite his or her reasons for not belonging to a union. Then write a report summarizing your findings and stating your conclusions about nonunion workers.

SUGGESTED READINGS

See the "Recommended Reading" listings on pages 599-600 of the textbook if you wish to explore further the material presented in this lesson.

SUGGESTED WEB SITES

Several places in the textbook will include information marked "The History Place." These are references to related web sites. See the "Suggested Web Sites" at the end of the chapters of the textbook if you wish to further explore the material presented in this lesson.

PRACTICE TEST

The following items will help you evaluate your understanding of this lesson. Use the answer key at the end of the lesson to check your answers or to locate material related in each question.

MULTIPLE-CHOICE INSTRUCTIONS

Choose the single best answer. If more than one answer is required, it will be so indicated.

1. An important factor influencing industrial work in late-nineteenth-century America was
    A. the decline of mass production.
    B. less demand for unskilled labor.
    C. cooperation between native-born and immigrant workers.
    D. ethnic diversity.

2. Workers in industrial America in the 1880s and 1890s
    A. tended to be wage earners rather than independent artisans.
    B. had to be skilled in order to get a job.
    C. faced a declining need for their labor.
    D. were similar to pre-Civil War numbers and types.

3. The workplace in industrial America of the 1880s and 1890s
    A. provided a safe environment.
    B. promoted the idea that a happy worker was productive.
    C. emphasized small shops rather than large factories.
    D. tended to divide workers from one another.

4. By the end of the nineteenth century, most working-class Americans
    A. enjoyed greater material comfort than European workers.
    B. demonstrated high levels of job skills.
    C. acquired steady employment.
    D. benefited from unemployment insurance.

5. Among the families of industrial workers during the late nineteenth century,
   A. white married women often worked outside the home.
   B. children were seldom expected to work.
   C. women were often limited in employment opportunities by ethnic tradition.
   D. domestic servants enjoyed the greatest freedom and benefits.

6. In the era between 1865 and 1900, American workers
   A. successfully unionized the majority of the work force.
   B. often protested against working conditions.
   C. passively accepted their working conditions.
   D. seldom used the strike.

7. The first major attempt to establish a national labor organization after the Civil War was made by the
   A. Congress for Industrial Organization.
   B. American Federation of Labor.
   C. Knights of Labor.
   D. National Labor Union.

8. According to the leaders of the American Federation of Labor, the main concern of a national union should be to
   A. organize workers in all trades.
   B. cooperate with employers to win concessions.
   C. use the political system to win concessions.
   D. focus on immediate, practical benefits.

9. Eugene Debs
   A. turned to socialism after the Pullman strike.
   B. forced George Pullman to make concessions in 1894.
   C. headed the AFL.
   D. organized the successful railway strike of 1877.

10. Most unions had little success in the late nineteenth century because
    A. workers had no interest in their fellow laborers.
    B. workforce size was declining.
    C. unionism ran counter to the tradition of individualism.
    D. government protection made unions unnecessary.

11. All of the following were associated with strike activity at the McCormick company in 1885-86 EXCEPT
    A. management's decision to cut wages.
    B. Irish influence in the molders union and city government.
    C. striking workers attacks on scabs and Pinkerton guards.
    D. Governor Altgeld's intervention on behalf of the union.

12. Workers were meeting in Haymarket Square on the night of May 4, 1886, in order to
    A. take over the McCormick factory.
    B. shut down a nearby police station.
    C. protest police actions of the previous day.
    D. organize an armed takeover of city government.

13. Anarchists were found guilty of murdering people at Haymarket Square in 1886 because
    A. they were all present when the bomb was thrown.
    B. the judge and jury were predisposed toward a guilty verdict.
    C. they were poorly defended.
    D. evidence showed that they were clearly responsible.

14. Large numbers of immigrant workers entered the United States in the late nineteenth century for all of the following reasons EXCEPT
    A. excess population growth in Europe.
    B. demand for laborers in the United States.
    C. recruitment of European workers by American labor unions.
    D. management profiting from cheap labor.

15. In the late nineteenth century, most business managers viewed their workers as
    A. worthy of safe and pleasant work environments.
    B. expendable commodities who could be easily replaced.
    C. radical anarchists threatening their property.
    D. equal partners in making decisions about the workplace.

16. Strikes in the late nineteenth century often failed for all of the following reasons EXCEPT
    A. government protection of the private property right of business owners.
    B. availability of surplus labor.
    C. radical domination of labor unions.
    D. strength and authority of management.

17. One reason why there was little public support for unions in the late nineteenth century was that
    A. unions were dominated by radical leaders.
    B. America was still largely a rural society.
    C. industrial workers did not believe in hard work.
    D. government protection made unions unnecessary.

ESSAY/PROBLEM QUESTIONS

18. Describe and explain the costs and benefits of industrialization as it related to the status of workers in the late nineteenth century. How did workers cope with their plight? What gains were made by workers? Why were these gains so limited?

19. Compare and contrast the Knights of Labor and the American Federation of Labor in terms of their philosophies, goals, leaders, and accomplishments. Which group was more successful? Why? Why did unions in general have a difficult time in the late nineteenth century?

ANSWER KEY

	Answers	Learning Objectives	Focus Points	References
1.	D	1	T1	Nash, p. 582
2.	A	1	T2	Nash, pp. 583-584
3.	D	1	T3	Nash, p. 584
4.	A	1	T4	Nash, pp. 585-586
5.	C	1	T5	Nash, p. 586
6.	B	2	T6	Nash, pp. 590-592
7.	D	2	T7	Nash, p. 592
8.	D	2	T8, V5	Nash, p. 594 and Video
9.	A	3	T9	Nash, p. 596
10.	C	4	T10, V5	Nash, p. 596 and Video
11.	D	3	R1	Reader
12.	C	3	R2	Reader
13.	B	3	R3	Reader
14.	C	1	V1	Video
15.	B	3	V2	Video
16.	C	3	V3	Video
17.	B	3	V4	Video
18.		All	All	Text, Reader, and Video
19.		All	All	Text, Reader, and Video

Lesson 4

The Huddled Masses

LESSON ASSIGNMENTS

Review the following assignments in order to schedule your time appropriately. Pay careful attention; the titles and numbers of the textbook chapter, the telecourse guide lesson, and the video program may be different from one another.

Text: Nash et al., *The American People, Volume Two: From 1865,*
          Chapter 18, "The Rise of Smokestack America," pp. 569-576; and
          Chapter 19, "Politics and Reform," pp. 609-619.

Video: "The Huddled Masses,"
          from the series *America in Perspective.*

OVERVIEW

Americans living at the present time are accustomed to urban life. While certainly not without its problems, that life may be better than that experienced by Americans of a century earlier. Much of what we take for granted was first experienced in the dynamic urban growth which accompanied industrialization. What was the lure of the city? Who were the people who came there? How did their hopes mesh or clash with the reality of urban America?

During the half century after the Civil War, the United States, along with much of Western Europe, experienced a remarkable urban growth. Although urban life had been part of the American experience from colonial times, as late as 1850 less than thirteen percent of Americans lived in cities. The pace of urbanization quickened so much after the Civil War that by 1920, more than half of the nation's people lived in cities. Obviously, the growth of cities was a by-product of the industrialization process which the United States underwent during that era. Concentration of industry demanded concentration of labor, and thus the cities expanded in keeping with the expansion of industry.

Ironically perhaps, the masses who peopled the American cities in the late nineteenth century came from the farm. The application of machinery to the tasks of agriculture helped spur productivity to such a level that not as many farmers were needed to support urban America. While the American farmers, or more likely their sons and daughters, took the road "into town," another route to the American cities was being taken by European immigrants. By the millions they came across the Atlantic Ocean in the late nineteenth and early twentieth centuries. The "new" immigrants, those from southern and eastern Europe and largely of peasant backgrounds, tended to settle in the city. The frontier in America was "closed" after 1890, and, besides, American industrialists were more than willing to employ this supply of cheap labor.

The most obvious magnet which drew Americans from their farms and immigrants from overseas and across borders was economic opportunity. The other causal factors which drew people to the city may be classified as psychological or social. Historian Arthur M. Schlesinger referred to these forces as the "lure of the city." The excitement, the noises, the variety, the "sinfulness"—all of these made the city strangely alluring.

While the city had its economic and psychological attractions, it also had its harsher sides. Crime and policing problems, traffic congestion, pollution, and housing shortages are not unique to our times. Jacob A. Riis, photographer and author of *How the Other Half Lives* (1890) publicized the inhuman living conditions in New York City's tenements. Crowded, filthy, and owned by absentee landlords, the tenements were breeding grounds for crime and disease. It was in the slums such as those described by Riis that many Americans experienced poverty personally and many others discovered that it existed in an industrialized and urbanized nation. As Jacob Riis asked, "What sort of answer, think you, would come from these tenements to the question 'Is life worth living?'"

Political bosses emerged to "help" the urban masses cope. Bosses did small but necessary favors for the urban poor in return for their votes. While the bosses did take the rough edges off of life for thousands of people, their corruption prompted urban political reformers to search for more honest and efficient ways to meet the needs of urban America. Even though most substantive political reform appeared in the early 1900s, social reformers began to act in the late nineteenth century. Jane Addams founded Hull House in Chicago in 1889, and other settlement houses were opened in other cities. At the same time, the Social Gospel movement linked salvation to social betterment. Meanwhile, most urbanites struggled to survive as best they could. While life could be hard, they, like the rest of us, hoped that their children would be better off and most of them were.

In summary, living conditions in the late-nineteenth-century city were harsh for most of the urban masses. They came, both from farms in the United States and from other nations, seeking new opportunities and hoping for the best. Like all of us, they had to face reality and cope as best they could. Finally, let us consider two thoughts from Alan Kraut's book, *The Huddled Masses: The Immigrant in American Society, 1880-1921* (Arlington Heights, Ill.: Harlan Davidson, 1982):

> The immigrant experience was neither romantic nor glamorous; many people starved, many retreated into taverns or insanity. But the great number of new immigrants made a success of their lives, mapping out goals according to their own specifications, making compromises with American society which they considered necessary. . . . [They] changed America even as they were changed by it. (p. 7)
>
> To fully understand immigration (and history, urban as well as the rest), one must listen to these personal stories. Ultimately, history is not made by huddled masses, or even triumphant cavalcades, but by specific individuals, weighing options, making compromises, squaring shoulders, having a joke, and muddling through. . . . (p. 185)

LEARNING OBJECTIVES

Goal—The purpose of this lesson is to increase our understanding of the causes and consequences of the rapid urbanization of the United States in the late nineteenth century.

Objectives—Upon completing this lesson, you should be able to:
1. Describe and explain why the population of American cities grew so rapidly in the post-Civil War era.
2. Assess the social and political consequences of this rapid urban growth.
3. Describe and explain the causes and consequences of the massive immigration of the era.
4. Examine how people coped with urban conditions, including the efforts of the urban reformers of that time.

TEXT FOCUS POINTS

The following questions are designed to help you get the most from your reading. Review them before you do your reading. After completing the assignment, write responses and/or notes to reinforce what you have learned.

Text: Nash et al., *The American People,* Chapter 18, pp. 569-576; and Chapter 19, pp. 609-619.

1. What accounted for the dramatic increase in urban population in the late nineteenth century?
2. How did novelists Theodore Dreiser and Stephen Crane depict life in the city?
3. What explains the increase in the number of immigrants, including Mexican and Chinese, entering the United States in the late nineteenth century? What distinguished "old immigrants" from "new immigrants"?
4. How and why was the industrial city geographically different from the pre-industrial (walking) city?
5. What were the characteristics of a working-class neighborhood, including the African-American neighborhoods of the North? How did these people cope?
6. How were upper- and middle-class neighborhoods different from the working-class neighborhoods? What were the effects of the geographic separation of the neighborhoods?
7. How did Henry George, reform Darwinists, and pragmatists provide a basis for urban reform?
8. Describe the philosophy and actions of the Settlement House and Social Gospel movements.
9. Describe the costs and benefits of the boss system. How did Samuel Jones try to reform the city?
10. How and why did the women's suffrage movement change course in the late nineteenth century?

The following questions are designed to help you get the most from the video segment of this lesson. Review them before you watch the video. After viewing the video segment, write responses and/or notes to reinforce what you have learned.

Video: "The Huddled Masses"

1. Why were people migrating to the cities? What usually determined where the immigrants would settle?
2. Describe the conditions found in the city. Why were conditions generally so bad?
3. How did immigrants and others living in American cities in the late nineteenth century cope with urban life?
4. Why did the urban bosses help the immigrants? Why were they criticized? Why were so many bosses Irish?
5. How did the Social Gospel and the Settlement House movements attempt to deal with urban problems? What limited the success of these efforts?

ENRICHMENT IDEAS

These activities are not required unless your instructor assigns them. They are offered as suggestions to help you learn more about the material presented in this lesson.

1. Imagine yourself to be an immigrant from Europe in the late nineteenth century. Write a two-page letter to relatives back home in which you describe housing, work, and opportunity in the United States. Would you tell them to join you or not?
2. If any of your relatives were immigrants to the United States in the late nineteenth or early twentieth centuries, investigate their experiences (use letters, photographs, etc.). Write a two-page report in which you describe their experiences.
3. Read *How the Other Half Lives* by Jacob Riis and then write a critical analysis of it in which you describe the main themes of the book and give a personal evaluation of it.

4. Read the article entitled "The First Chapter of Children's Rights" in *Perspectives on America, Volume 2.* Then write a 750-word essay in which you summarize the article and what it indicates about the role of government in family matters.

5. Read the "Technology Changes the American People" segment about the bicycles on pages 614-615 in your textbook. Write a 750-word essay discussing social change and the bicycle. What were some of the cultural activities it affected?

SUGGESTED READINGS

See the "Recommended Reading" listings on pages 599-600 and pages 630-631 of the text if you wish to explore further the material presented in this lesson.

SUGGESTED WEB SITES

Several places in the textbook will include information marked "The History Place." These are references to related web sites. See the "Suggested Web Sites" at the end of the chapters of the textbook if you wish to further explore the material presented in this lesson.

PRACTICE TEST

The following items will help you evaluate your understanding of this lesson. Use the answer key at the end of the lesson to check your answers or to locate material related in each question.

MULTIPLE-CHOICE INSTRUCTIONS

Select the single best answer. If more than one answer is required, it will be so indicated.

1. A major consequence of industrialization in the United States was an increase in
   A. the size of the American family.
   B. migration from the city to the farm.
   C. emigration from the United States.
   D. the population of American cities.

2. The "new immigrants," whose migration to the United States increased after 1880, came mainly from
   A. China.
   B. Southeast Asia.
   C. northern and western Europe.
   D. southern and eastern Europe.

3. Living arrangements in the industrial city differed from the pre-industrial (walking) city in that
   A. neighborhoods tended to be more segregated by race and class.
   B. industrial districts tended to be located in the suburbs.
   C. people with varied backgrounds and incomes lived side by side.
   D. less pollution occurred in the industrial city.

4. Black Americans who lived in the North between 1865 and 1900
   A. shared full economic opportunity with northern whites.
   B. abandoned religious institutions in their new urban setting.
   C. generally faced wretched living conditions.
   D. achieved little professional or artistic success because of prejudice.

5. Upper- and middle-class neighborhoods of the late nineteenth century tended to be
   A. located away from the central business district.
   B. clustered near the downtown skyscrapers.
   C. relatively well integrated.
   D. populated mostly by factory workers.

6. The primary purpose of the Settlement House movement was to
   A. elect Jane Addams to the U.S. Senate.
   B. convert immigrants to Christianity.
   C. promote the issue of voting rights for women.
   D. help immigrant families adapt to urban living.

7. In the late nineteenth century, urban political bosses
   A. supported the Settlement House movement.
   B. advocated the preaching of the Social Gospel.
   C. received support from middle-class urban reformers.
   D. obtained votes by doing favors for immigrants.

8. In the late nineteenth century, advocates for the right of women to vote
   A. had no valid reason for wanting the ballot.
   B. supported a radical program of religious and social reform.
   C. focused on such expedient arguments as countering the vote of immigrant men.
   D. united behind the leadership of Elizabeth Cady Stanton.

9. Living conditions in American cities in the late nineteenth century were deplorable for the poor for all of the following reasons EXCEPT
   A. many were strangers to the city.
   B. housing arrangements were crowded.
   C. city services were inadequate.
   D. a sense of community was lacking in ethnic neighborhoods.

10. Immigrants living in American cities in the late nineteenth century coped with harsh conditions by
   A. accepting blacks into their neighborhoods.
   B. lobbying to abolish child labor.
   C. moving immediately to the suburbs.
   D. engaging in community activities.

ESSAY/PROBLEM QUESTION

11. Describe and explain the causes and consequences of the rapid urbanization of the United States in the late nineteenth century. How did urban people cope with the urban conditions of that era?

ANSWER KEY

	Answers	Learning Objectives	Focus Points	References
1.	D	1	T1, V1	Nash, p. 570 and Video
2.	D	3	T3	Nash, p. 571
3.	A	2	T4	Nash, pp. 574-575
4.	C	4	T5	Nash, p. 575
5.	A	2	T6	Nash, p. 576
6.	D	4	T8, V5	Nash, p. 612 and Video
7.	D	4	T9, V4	Nash, pp. 616-617 and Video
8.	C	4	T10	Nash, p. 619
9.	D	2	V2	Video
10.	D	4	V3	Video
11.		All	All	Text and Video

Lesson 5

The American Dream Deferred

LESSON ASSIGNMENTS

Review the following assignments in order to schedule your time appropriately. Pay careful attention; the titles and numbers of the textbook chapter, the telecourse guide lesson, and the video program may be different from one another.

Text: Nash et al., *The American People, Volume Two: From 1865,* Chapter 17, "The Realities of Rural America," pp. 547-553.

Reader: *Perspectives on America, Volume 2,* "Ride-in: A Century of Protest Begins," by Alan F. Westin.

Video: "The American Dream Deferred," from the series *America in Perspective.*

OVERVIEW

While the majority of Americans attempted to cope with the changes associated with the emerging industrial nation, minorities faced even greater challenges. In some ways these challenges were not new, for the historical experience of minorities in the United States has always provided the most severe test of the very principles upon which the nation was founded. Prior to the Civil War, enslavement of African Americans was the most obvious denial of equality. At the same time, free blacks and other minorities, including women and practically anyone who was not a white Anglo-Saxon Protestant (WASP), faced some sort of discrimination. Since the Civil War, the struggle to establish equal rights has continued, and in many ways, the status of minorities remains a test of our nation even today.

At the end of Reconstruction (1877), African Americans were about to enter a period in their history which black historian Rayford Logan long ago termed the "betrayal of the Negro." The dream of equal rights fostered by the constitutional amendments and federal legislation passed during the Reconstruction era was shattered by the realities of racism, terrorism, and legal restrictions. When the Supreme Court in the *Plessy* decision (1896) approved "separate but equal" facilities, it sanctioned a segregated society that was not equal. For the next fifty-eight years, black citizens in the United States would not have equal rights, let alone equal social and economic opportunities.

Analysis of the responses of African Americans and their leaders to their plight in the late nineteenth century provides us with an opportunity to ponder how one copes with inequality and brings about a more just society. On the one hand, Booker T. Washington advocated an approach which emphasized self-help; on the other, W. E. B. Du Bois wanted to challenge segregation and discrimination directly through political and legal means. These two approaches are not mutually exclusive, and they still have a great deal of relevance a century later.

Although the primary focus of this lesson concerns the African-American minority, other groups faced clear discrimination in the late nineteenth century. For Hispanics, especially those in the southwestern United States, rights were denied. For Asians, hostility was so great that the Chinese were barred from entering the United States after 1882. Women of every race and ethnic group faced some of the discrimination directed particularly at African Americans, Hispanics, and Asians. Most obviously, women were denied the right to vote in most states. Also remember that this was the era in which the Plains Indians were devastated. (See Lesson 1.)

In summary, the late nineteenth century was a very difficult time for most minorities in the United States. The hopes and promises of the American Dream were deferred, and Americans in the twentieth century would have to live with the consequences.

LEARNING OBJECTIVES

Goal—The purpose of this lesson is to increase our understanding of how and why American minorities, particularly African Americans, were denied equality and how they responded to their plight.

Objectives—Upon completing this lesson, you should be able to:
1. Describe and explain how and why African Americans faced discrimination and were denied equality in the late nineteenth century.
2. Analyze the responses of African Americans, particularly as expressed by recognized black leaders, to their plight.

3. Describe and explain the status of minorities in general at the end of the nineteenth century, and assess the long-term significance of that status.

TEXT FOCUS POINTS

The following questions are designed to help you get the most from your reading. Review them before you do your reading. After completing the assignment, write responses and/or notes to reinforce what you have learned.

Text: Nash et al., *The American People,* Chapter 17, pp. 547-553.

1. What was meant by the term "New South"?
2. How much change really took place in the South in the late nineteenth century? What limited change?
3. How and why had blacks, particularly in the South, been subjected to second-class citizenship by 1900? What was the importance of the 1896 *Plessy v. Ferguson* Supreme Court decision?
4. What responses were made by black leaders to the conditions facing blacks in the late nineteenth and early twentieth centuries? Distinguish between the approaches taken by Booker T. Washington and W. E. B. Du Bois.

READER FOCUS POINTS

Reader: *Perspectives on America, Volume 2,* "Ride-in: A Century of Protest Begins," by Westin.

1. Why did Congress pass the Civil Rights Act of 1875 (Sumner's Law)? What were its provisions? What was the reaction to the law?
2. Explain the Supreme Court's decision in the "Civil Rights Cases" (1883). Why did Justice John Marshall Harlan dissent? What was the significance of the Supreme Court's ruling?

VIDEO FOCUS POINTS

The following questions are designed to help you get the most from the video segment of this lesson. Review them before you watch the video. After viewing the video segment, write responses and/or notes to reinforce what you have learned.

Video: "The American Dream Deferred"

1. Describe the status of African Americans, Hispanics, Chinese, and women in the United States in the late nineteenth century.
2. How and why were African Americans denied equality in the late nineteenth century?
3. Compare and contrast the views of Booker T. Washington and W. E. B. Du Bois. Who was more successful in the late nineteenth and early twentieth centuries? Why?
4. What is the long-term significance of the approaches advocated by Booker T. Washington and W. E. B. Du Bois?
5. How do the struggles of minorities today parallel the struggles of minorities in the late nineteenth century?

ENRICHMENT IDEAS

These activities are not required unless your instructor assigns them. They are offered as suggestions to help you learn more about the material presented in this lesson.

1. In a well-reasoned, 750-word essay, defend the approach taken by either Booker T. Washington or W. E. B. Du Bois to the conditions facing African Americans in the late nineteenth and early twentieth centuries. At the end of your essay, please comment on the relevance of the approach you have defended to minority issues today.
2. You are a black sharecropper in the South in 1898. Write a 750-word letter to a friend in which you describe your economic, social, and political status and what you plan to do to change it.

SUGGESTED READINGS

See the "Recommended Reading" listings on page 559 of the text if you wish to explore further the material presented in this lesson.

SUGGESTED WEB SITES

Several places in the textbook will include information marked "The History Place." This is a reference to a related web site. See the "Suggested Web Sites" at the end of the chapter of the textbook if you wish to further explore the material presented in this lesson.

PRACTICE TEST

The following items will help you evaluate your understanding of this lesson. Use the answer key at the end of the lesson to check your answers or to locate material related in each question.

MULTIPLE-CHOICE INSTRUCTIONS

Choose the single best answer. If more than one answer is required, it will be so indicated.

1. "New South" advocates
    A. urged the South to increase the production of cotton.
    B. believed the South should be self-sufficient.
    C. rejected entrepreneurial values.
    D. refused northern dollars for southern development.

2. By 1890, the South had
    A. reaped many of the benefits of industrialization.
    B. rejected all of its older values.
    C. improved its economic position in manufacturing relative to the North.
    D. remained economically dependent on the North.

3. According to the *Plessy v. Ferguson* decision,
   A. separate facilities for African Americans and whites were illegal.
   B. segregation laws violated the Fourteenth Amendment.
   C. African-American voters could be disenfranchised through the "good character" clause.
   D. "separate but equal" accommodations were constitutional.

4. In the late nineteenth century, all of the following factors combined to deny African Americans equality EXCEPT
   A. repeal of the Fourteenth Amendment.
   B. terrorist acts like lynchings.
   C. sharecropper systems in agriculture.
   D. poll taxes and grandfather clauses.

5. Booker T. Washington
   A. argued for immediate social equality for African Americans.
   B. reinforced a movement toward black militancy.
   C. advocated a moderate self-help program for blacks.
   D. alienated white leaders.

6. The Civil Rights Act of 1875 (Sumner's Law) said that citizens had the right to
   A. vote even if they were ex-Confederate officers.
   B. maintain a policy of "one man, one vote."
   C. refuse service to anyone.
   D. equal enjoyment of public accommodations.

7. The significance of the Supreme Court's ruling on the Civil Rights Act of 1875 was that it
   A. destroyed the progress made toward integration in the 1870s and 1880s.
   B. diminished the rights of property owners.
   C. upheld the continued disenfranchisement of southern whites.
   D. perpetuated the corruption in reconstruction programs.

8. An obvious denial of equality in the late nineteenth century was demonstrated by the fact that women could not
   A. own personal property.
   B. vote in all states.
   C. exercise the right of free speech.
   D. enroll in colleges.

9. One significant long-term effect of W. E. B. Du Bois' approach to African-American problems can be found in his creation of a

   A. program for vocational education.
   B. campaign for equal rights.
   C. back-to-Africa movement.
   D. violent protest organization.

10. In the video program, Professor Darlene Clark Hine found parallels between the struggles of minorities today and those of one hundred years ago in all of the following areas EXCEPT

    A. respect for cultural differences.
    B. access to quality social services.
    C. denial of opportunities to vote.
    D. fair compensation for work.

ESSAY/PROBLEM QUESTIONS

11. Compare and contrast the philosophies and actions taken by Booker T. Washington and W. E. B. Du Bois. Whose approach do you think was the better one? Why?

12. Describe and explain how and why African Americans, despite the gains and promises made during the Reconstruction era, were subjected to an inferior position in American life by 1900. In your answer, be sure to include an analysis of the economic, social, and political status of African Americans.

ANSWER KEY

Answers	Learning Objectives	Focus Points	References
1. B	1	T1	Nash, p. 547
2. D	1	T2	Nash, pp. 547-548
3. D	1	T3, V2	Nash, p. 551 and Video
4. A	1	V2	Video
5. C	2	T4, V3	Nash, p. 553 and Video
6. D	1	R1	Reader
7. A	1	R2	Reader
8. B	3	V1	Video
9. B	2	V4	Video
10. C	3	V5	Video
11.	All	All	Text, Reader, and Video
12.	All	All	Text, Reader, and Video

Lesson 6

The Populist Challenge

LESSON ASSIGNMENTS

Review the following assignments in order to schedule your time appropriately. Pay careful attention; the titles and numbers of the textbook chapter, the telecourse guide lesson, and the video program may be different from one another.

Text: Nash et al., *The American People, Volume Two: From 1865,*
        Chapter 17, "The Realities of Rural America," pp. 553-560; and
        Chapter 19, "Politics and Reform," pp. 602-609, 619-625, and 628-631.

Reader: *Perspectives on America, Volume 2,*
        "Populism and Modern American Politics," by Peter Frederick.

Video: "The Populist Challenge,"
        from the series *America in Perspective.*

OVERVIEW

Americans living near the end of the twentieth century are accustomed to the rather pervasive presence of government in their lives. It is hard to imagine a time when the various local, state, and national government entities were not actively intervening in social and economic matters. The political debate today is not *if* governments are going to be involved, but to what extent. To understand why governments became activist, we must examine the initial political responses to industrialism made a century ago.

As the United States became more industrialized, concentration of people, resources, wealth, and political power became more apparent. The individual became less significant in the overall scheme of things unless, of course, an individual happened to be among the fortunate few who accumulated great wealth. The overwhelming majority of Americans, however, did not experience the power which great wealth can bestow. In a political system which was supposed to ensure that all votes counted the same, it became obvious that the very rich had much more political influence than the ordinary people.

From 1876 until the mid-1890s, national politics was hardly issue-oriented. This did not mean that issues were not present, for industrialization raised serious questions regarding tariffs, trust regulation, working conditions for laborers, and a whole series of farmer-related grievances concerning currency, prices, credit, railroads, and marketing agencies. Rather, it was an era in which the major parties and their standard-bearers chose to avoid the issues or to adopt a safe, middle-of-the-road position.

As in other periods in the political history of the United States, it was up to third parties, meaning any organized political structure other than the Republicans and Democrats, to push political reform. Most active in the late nineteenth century were the agrarian-dominated parties which demanded governmental action to control the big business interests and to provide their supporters with relief from economic distress. Although most of their ideas were at first rejected, many of them were taken over by a major party and enacted into law.

The most significant third party of the era was the Populist (or People's) Party. This organization and its leaders have been the subject of much historical analysis. Most significantly, the Populists challenged three ideologies which prevailed in the late nineteenth century: the success (or Alger) myth; social Darwinism; and "laissez-faire," the philosophy that government should leave business alone. In many ways it was a class movement, questioning whether industrial capitalism was serving human needs. (See Norman Pollack's *The Populist Response to Industrial America, American Midwestern Populist Thought*, New York: Norton and Company, 1962, p. 16.) It was a moment of egalitarian hope, of promise, not of triumph. Historian Lawrence Goodwyn has observed that today the values and sheer power of corporate America control employees, determine modes and style of mass communication and mass education, fashion American foreign policy, and shape the rules of the American political process. He states: "corporate values define modern American culture . . . . It was the corporate state that the People's Party attempted to bring under democratic control." ("The Irony of Populism," in *Perspectives on the American Past*, Glenview, Ill: Scott, Foresman, and Company, 1989, p. 153)

Armed with their far-reaching goals and their reform proposals, the Populists waged an effective campaign in 1892. Cutting across racial lines in the South and appealing to common economic interests, they appeared to be a potential threat to the established political order. When a severe depression hit the nation shortly after

Democrat Grover Cleveland's inauguration in 1893, the Populists seemed to pick up more momentum.

As the hard times persisted, the nation looked toward the 1896 presidential election in search of someone to lead the country back to prosperity. The Republicans had the advantage of not holding the presidency during the depression, and they nominated the "safe and sane" William McKinley to carry their pro-business banner. Meanwhile, the Democrats had greater problems and chose to take greater risks. Nominating William Jennings Bryan and adopting many of the Populist proposals as their own, they offered a clear alternative to the voters. The actions of the Democrats left the Populists with no real choice but to fuse with the Democrats and nominate Bryan. Although criticized by some purists as a conservative sellout, most Populists reasoned that fusion with the Democrats provided the only realistic chance to advance their issues. Such is the fate of a third party in the American political system.

The McKinley-Bryan contest in 1896 was the most significant presidential election between 1880 and 1912. It reflected the divisions taking place in a nation experiencing industrialization. Bryan and his appeal represented an America in which the happy yeoman shared in the opportunities available. McKinley stood for industry and commerce, an appeal to the new opportunities for the self-made man. McKinley and industry had won. But the ideas espoused by Bryan, and earlier the Populists, were applicable to more than an older, rural America. They had identified fundamental issues and proposed governmental intervention to deal with them. The issues would not die, and their proposed solutions would be championed by other reformers in other times.

LEARNING OBJECTIVES

Goal—The purpose of this lesson is to increase our understanding of how and why political leaders, political parties, and the political system in general responded to the newly industrialized nation.

Objectives—Upon completion of this lesson, you should be able to:
1. Analyze the economic and political concerns of rural Americans in the late nineteenth century and how farm organizations proposed to address those issues.
2. Describe and explain the characteristics of national politics during the late nineteenth century.
3. Describe and explain the rise and fall of the Populist party.

4. Assess the significance of the presidential election of 1896.

TEXT FOCUS POINTS

The following questions are designed to help you get the most from your reading. Review them before you do your reading. After completing the assignment, write responses and/or notes to reinforce what you have learned.

Text: Nash et al., *The American People,* Chapter 17, pp. 553-560; and Chapter 19, pp. 602-609, 619-625, and 628-631.

1. What were the goals of the National Grange and its members?
2. What factors limited the effectiveness of the Interstate Commerce Act?
3. Why were farmers in debt? How did the Alliance Movement address the debt problem as well as other grievances of the farmers? What positions did the Farmers' Alliance take in the Ocala platform (1890)?
4. What was the significance of the Populist party platform (1892)? Assess the success of the Populist party in 1892.
5. What characterized "Gilded Age" politics?
6. What were the major national issues of the era?
7. Why were voting percentages so high? Why were certain groups attracted to either the Republican or Democratic party?
8. What made the 1890s a "pivotal" decade in American politics?
9. What were the causes and consequences of the depression of 1893?
10. How did the presidential election of 1896 signify a turning point in American politics?

READER FOCUS POINTS

Reader: *Perspectives on America, Volume 2,* "Populism and Modern American Politics," by Frederick.

1. Why did the Populists pose a threat to the political and economic establishment in 1892? How successful were they in the elections of that year? What limited their success?
2. Why did the Populist party endorse William Jennings Bryan in 1896? What were the results of that decision?
3. Why does Professor Frederick refer to the election of 1896 as "one of the more significant elections in the history of American politics."
4. What was the legacy of the Populist party?
5. What does the Populist experience show us about political change in America?

VIDEO FOCUS POINTS

The following questions are designed to help you get the most from the video segment of this lesson. Review them before you watch the video. After viewing the video segment, write responses and/or notes to reinforce what you have learned.

Video: "The Populist Challenge"

1. Why did farmers emerge to press for political change in the late nineteenth century?
2. Who were the leaders of the Populist party? Who supported the Populist party?
3. How did the economic depression of the mid-1890s affect American politics?
4. Why did William McKinley win the presidential election of 1896? How did that election help shape the philosophy and composition of the two major parties?
5. In the final analysis, how successful were the Populists? What limited their success?

ENRICHMENT IDEAS

These activities are not required unless your instructor assigns them. They are offered as suggestions to help you learn more about the material presented in this lesson.

1. Read and analyze the "Recovering the Past" segment on pp. 626-627 of *The American People*. Write a report on that segment in which you answer the questions presented in the text.
2. Which side would you have been on in the 1896 election? Write a 750-word essay in which you explain and defend your position.

SUGGESTED READINGS

See the "Recommended Reading" listings on page 559 and pages 630-631 of the text if you wish to explore further the material presented in this lesson.

SUGGESTED WEB SITES

Several places in the textbook will include information marked "The History Place." These are references to related web sites. See the "Suggested Web Sites" at the end of the chapters of the textbook if you wish to further explore the material presented in this lesson.

PRACTICE TEST

The following items will help you evaluate your understanding of this lesson. Use the answer key at the end of the lesson to check your answers or to locate material related in each question.

MULTIPLE-CHOICE INSTRUCTIONS

Choose the single best answer. If more than one answer is required, it will be so indicated.

1. One of the primary goals of Grange members during the late nineteenth century was
   A. limitations on crop production.
   B. support for a deflationary monetary policy.
   C. maintenance of the gold standard.
   D. regulation of the railroads.

2. Among the factors which limited the effectiveness of the Interstate Commerce Act was lack of
   A. a federal regulatory agency.
   B. support from farm organizations.
   C. adequate enforcement power.
   D. meaningful state regulation of the railroads.

3. All of the following were reasons why farmers tended to be in debt in the 1880s and 1890s EXCEPT
   A. farm cooperatives greatly increased costs.
   B. prices for farm products fell.
   C. a national currency shortage existed.
   D. farmers paid very high mortgage interest rates.

4. The Populist party platform (1892) advocated all of the following EXCEPT
   A. more direct democracy.
   B. price supports for farm products.
   C. a graduated income tax.
   D. government ownership of railroads.

5. Between 1865 and 1900, national political leaders
    A. generally responded to the needs of the working class.
    B. primarily focused on the human problems of American society.
    C. frequently bolstered the interests of the rich.
    D. effectively solved problems confronting the American farmer.

6. Among the issues confronting American political leaders in the last three decades of the nineteenth century was
    A. secession.
    B. tariff revision.
    C. inflationary economy.
    D. scarcity of silver.

7. In the last three decades of the nineteenth century, American voters were generally
    A. uninterested in political participation.
    B. offended by emotional political appeals.
    C. interested in local issues.
    D. descendants of Revolutionary War families.

8. All of the following factors helped make the 1890s a "pivotal" decade in American politics EXCEPT
    A. the populations were changing from rural to urban.
    B. the quality of political leadership had never been higher.
    C. rapid industrialization brought major changes in the workplace.
    D. large immigration and internal migrations made people uneasy.

9. Agricultural and industrial overproduction during the late nineteenth century in the United States contributed to
    A. a decrease in american exports.
    B. financial panic.
    C. an increased capital for investment.
    D. an increase in the money supply.

10. One political result of the depression of 1893 was that
    A. President Cleveland was not renominated.
    B. income tax proposals disappeared.
    C. Populists would attract little interest in their ideas.
    D. Socialists would receive millions of votes in the next election.

---

11. A central issue in the election of 1896 was the question of
    A. tariff revision.
    B. civil service reform.
    C. civil rights.
    D. monetary policy.

12. The Populists posed a threat to the political and economic establishment in 1892 because they
    A. advocated socialism.
    B. forced issues onto the national political agenda.
    C. supported labor unions.
    D. demanded that "Jim Crow" laws be abolished.

13. In the reading, Professor Peter Frederick characterized the Populist decision to endorse Bryan in 1896 as
    A. wise in light of the circumstances.
    B. practical if they hoped to win.
    C. costly to the Democrats' chances for victory.
    D. disastrous for their future.

14. The election of 1896 showed the importance of
    A. selecting a popular vice presidential nominee.
    B. avoiding a real discussion of the issues.
    C. spending vast sums of money on a campaign.
    D. traveling throughout the nation if you hope to win.

15. Part of the legacy of the Populist party was that it
    A. established the agenda for American politics for twenty years.
    B. proved that third parties could have no influence.
    C. created opportunity for Republican success in the South.
    D. played a key role in the Democrats' control of urban politics.

16. The Populist experience showed us that
    A. significant political change occurs often.
    B. serious structural change is almost impossible.
    C. reform proposals usually help the poor gain power.
    D. third-party movements are unimportant in American politics.

17. Farmers began pressing for political change in the late nineteenth century because
    A. government price supports were too low.
    B. agricultural productivity had declined.
    C. major parties did not respond to their grievances.
    D. railroads refused to sell their excess land.

ESSAY/PROBLEM QUESTIONS

18. Why were the grievances of farmers generally being ignored in the late nineteenth century? How did they propose to bring about redress of their grievances? What did their efforts teach us about political change in America?

19. Describe and explain the significance of the 1896 presidential election in terms of the following four points: (a) candidates, (b) issues, (c) campaigns, (d) results.

ANSWER KEY

	Answers	Learning Objectives	Focus Points	References
1.	D	1	T1	Nash, p. 554
2.	C	1	T2	Nash, pp. 554-555
3.	A	1	T3	Nash, p. 554
4.	B	3	T4, V2	Nash, pp. 557-558 and Video
5.	C	2	T5	Nash, pp. 604-605
6.	B	2	T6	Nash, p. 606
7.	C	2	T7	Nash, pp. 607-609
8.	B	3	T8	Nash, pp. 619-620
9.	B	3	T9	Nash, pp. 621-624
10.	A	3	V3	Video
11.	D	4	T10	Nash, pp. 624-625
12.	B	3	R1	Reader
13.	D	3	R2	Reader
14.	C	4	R3, V4	Reader and Video
15.	A	3	R4, V5	Reader and Video
16.	B	3	R5	Reader
17.	C	1	V1	Video
18.		All	All	Text, Reader, and Video
19.		All	All	Text, Reader, and Video

Lesson 7

War and Empire

LESSON ASSIGNMENTS

Review the following assignments in order to schedule your time appropriately. Pay careful attention; the titles and numbers of the textbook chapter, the telecourse guide lesson, and the video program may be different from one another.

Text: Nash et al., *The American People, Volume Two: From 1865*, Chapter 20, "Becoming a World Power," pp. 632-648.

Video: "War and Empire," from the series *America in Perspective*.

OVERVIEW

Recognition of the United States as a world power, taken for granted by Americans living today, is a relatively recent historical development. Prior to 1898, the United States had not played a particularly active role in the world arena. There had been occasional forays of diplomatic activity, but most of those concerned boundary settlements or the occasional acquisition of additional territory. For the most part, the policymakers in the United States were content to follow the sagacious advice of George Washington and Thomas Jefferson and let the world go its own way. Besides, there were enough domestic issues to be dealt with, including the expansion of the West and the development of the industrial potential of the country. Thus, until near the end of the nineteenth century, the United States was basically isolationist in the diplomatic and military sense of that term.

Ironically perhaps, some of the same forces which propelled the United States to settle the last domestic frontier and to become an industrial giant thrust the nation onto the world scene in the 1890s. For example, if it was the "Manifest Destiny" of the United States to spread democracy and Christianity across the country, why should such a mission stop at the nation's borders? Could not industries use overseas markets and resources? Should not such a powerful industrial nation take its place among the leading military powers of the world?

In 1898 regular American troops fought outside North America in a declared war for the first time in U.S. history. The necessity of this war with Spain has been questioned, for no vital interest to the United States was at stake. That being the case, the Spanish-American War offers an interesting and enlightening study of how and why seemingly minor factors can push a nation into war. It can also provide us with a frame of reference from which we can analyze the causes of wars in general.

Furthermore, when the United States entered the Spanish-American War, few people had given much thought to its consequences. As a result of the war, the United States was in a position to acquire an overseas empire and join the major European powers in the great game of imperialism. The decision to engage in imperialism, debated in the U.S. Senate when the question of ratification of the peace treaty was discussed, raised fundamental questions about the role of the United States in the world. Essentially the same questions, many of which relate to a tense mixture of self-interest and idealism, are still being discussed a hundred years later. Lastly, the suppression of the Filipinos not only illustrated the economic, physical, and ideological costs of empire, but also indicated the difficulties of fighting an undeclared war thousands of miles from the United States against a people seeking their national identity.

Since this particular lesson concludes a set of seven lessons covering the period 1877-1900, a few summary thoughts as well as a few projections are in order. Looking backward from 1900, how remarkable the changes must have appeared. The frontier had been closed, and a long chapter in the centuries-old cultural clash between the American Indians and non-Indians had ended. The settlers who had moved West also faced hardship and disillusionment, and eventually they joined other farmers in leading a political movement to challenge the newly dominant corporate powers. President McKinley's election victories in 1896 and 1900, however, seemed to indicate that industry had triumphed both politically and economically. Likewise, the victory by the United States in the "splendid little war" and the decision to engage in imperialism opened up even broader horizons for the nation's "Manifest Destiny." Looking forward, the United States was now in a position to extend its economic, political, and socio-cultural influence throughout the world in the twentieth century. At the same time, the problems associated with the urban industrial nation needed to be addressed if all Americans would have a legitimate chance to pursue the American Dream at home.

LEARNING OBJECTIVES

Goal—The purpose of this lesson is to increase our understanding of why the United States entered the Spanish-American War and our understanding of the costs and benefits of establishing an overseas empire.

Objectives—Upon completing this lesson, you should be able to:
1. Analyze the major factors which contributed to a shift in U.S. foreign policy in the late nineteenth century.
2. Examine the underlying and immediate causes of the Spanish-American War, as well as the immediate consequences of that war.
3. Analyze the positions of those favoring and those opposing imperialism.
4. Assess the initial costs and benefits of the decision for empire.

TEXT FOCUS POINTS

The following questions are designed to help you get the most from your reading. Review them before you do your reading. After completing the assignment, write responses and/or notes to reinforce what you have learned.

Text: Nash et al., *The American People,* Chapter 20, pp. 632-648.

1. Prior to the mid-1890s, what factors encouraged U.S. interests beyond its borders? What factors limited U.S. interests?
2. How did industrial growth in the United States in the late nineteenth century promote a shift in U.S. foreign policy?
3. What were the views of Theodore Roosevelt, Henry Cabot Lodge, and Alfred T. Mahan regarding the role of the United States in the world? How did they influence policy decisions?
4. What explains the "missionary impulse" of the United States in the late nineteenth century? Where were Protestant missionaries most active?
5. What affected public opinion and how important was public opinion in foreign policy decisions?
6. What were the "fundamental" (underlying) causes of the Spanish-American War? What "events" (immediate causes) sparked the outbreak of hostilities? What was the significance of the Teller Amendment?

7. Why did Secretary of State John Hay call the Spanish-American War "a splendid little war"? Was he correct?

8. What were the arguments for and against annexation of the Philippines? In what ways did the "Filipino-American War" reveal some "hypocrisies" in U.S. policy?

9. What was the significance of the "insular cases?"

10. Why did the McKinley-Roosevelt ticket win the presidential election of 1900? What was the significance of their victory?

VIDEO FOCUS POINTS

The following questions are designed to help you get the most from the video segment of this lesson. Review them before you watch the video. After viewing the video segment, write responses and/or notes to reinforce what you have learned.

Video: "War and Empire"

1. How did the major economic, social, and political developments of the late nineteenth century affect the relationship of the United States with the rest of the world?

2. What was William McKinley's role in bringing the United States into war with Spain?

3. Why did Commodore George Dewey attack the Spanish fleet in the Philippines? What was the significance of his victory?

4. Why did American actions in the Philippines from 1898 to 1902 raise questions about the nation's ideals?

5. What were the costs and benefits of American control of the Philippines?

ENRICHMENT IDEAS

These activities are not required unless your instructor assigns them. They are offered as suggestions to help you learn more abut the material presented in this lesson.

1. You are a member of the Congress of the United States in the spring of 1898. You have just voted on the declaration of war against Spain. Write a 750-word essay in which you explain to your constituents the reasons you voted as you did.
2. Read the quotes from President McKinley and Senator Hoar found on pages 645-646 of *The American People* text. Write a 750-word essay in which you explain why you agree with one position and disagree with the other.
3. You are a Filipino nationalist in 1899. Write a 750-word article, which you intend to publish in a U.S. newspaper, in which you express your views on the actions of the United States in the Philippines and your recommendations to U.S. policymakers.
4. Read the article entitled, "The Needless War With Spain," in *Perspectives on America, Volume 2*. Then write a 750-word essay in which you summarize the article and analyze the perspective presented by the author.

SUGGESTED READINGS

See the "Recommended Reading" listings on page 660 of the text if you wish to explore further the material presented in this lesson.

SUGGESTED WEB SITES

Several places in the textbook will include information marked "The History Place." This is a reference to a related web site. See the "Suggested Web Sites" at the end of the chapter of the textbook if you wish to further explore the material presented in this lesson.

PRACTICE TEST

The following items will help you evaluate your understanding of this lesson. Use the answer key at the end of the lesson to check your answers or to locate material related in each question.

MULTIPLE-CHOICE INSTRUCTIONS

Choose the single best answer. If more than one answer is required, it will be so indicated.

1. During the first hundred years after independence, American foreign policy was concerned primarily with
   A. continental expansion.
   B. imperialism.
   C. transatlantic commercial trade.
   D. national armament.

2. One of the factors that promoted America's search for new markets between 1865 and 1900 was the
   A. increase in domestic consumption.
   B. decline in demand for American goods abroad.
   C. overproduction of industrial and agricultural goods.
   D. depression of 1893.

3. During the 1890s, a group led by Theodore Roosevelt and Henry Cabot Lodge
   A. opposed American expansion outside the western hemisphere.
   B. promoted a highly nationalistic foreign policy.
   C. endorsed a policy of "continentalism."
   D. encouraged Bryan's anti-imperialistic concepts.

4. A location emphasized by Christian missionaries in the late nineteenth century was
   A. Europe.
   B. Latin America.
   C. Africa.
   D. China.

5. In the late nineteenth century, politicians began to realize that events occurring overseas could do all of the following EXCEPT
    A. rejuvenate national self-confidence.
    B. restore patriotic pride.
    C. possibly win votes.
    D. solve the nation's domestic problems.

6. A fundamental cause of the Spanish-American War was the
    A. heroic actions of Cuban exiles.
    B. American public's concern for the Cuban people.
    C. action of the Assistant Secretary of the Navy, Theodore Roosevelt.
    D. accurate reporting by the yellow press.

7. During the Spanish-American War, the United States
    A. faced a major military challenge.
    B. defeated Spain relatively easily.
    C. attacked Japan.
    D. failed in most battles with the Spanish navy.

8. The major argument used by those who opposed annexation of the Philippines was that annexation would
    A. contradict the republican traditions of the United States.
    B. violate Christian ethics.
    C. anger Filipinos who opposed American rule.
    D. retard America's economic growth.

9. In the "insular cases," the Supreme Court determined that
    A. all people living under American control could enjoy the same rights and privileges.
    B. some people under American control could be treated differently than others.
    C. no people under American control could be denied citizenship.
    D. Hawaiians and Puerto Ricans could enjoy full rights of American citizenship but Filipinos could not.

10. In the election of 1900, the public
    A. rejected McKinley's foreign policy.
    B. endorsed Bryan's foreign policy.
    C. supported McKinley's decision to annex the Philippines.
    D. supported Bryan's attempt to make currency the major issue.

11. In the video program, Professor Robert Beisner's discussion of the Spanish-American War suggested that President McKinley
    A. delegated major decisions to Theodore Roosevelt.
    B. played a vital role in the American entry.
    C. allowed public opinion to sway him too much.
    D. matched the description provided in Ambassador DeLome's letter.

12. Commodore George Dewey's victory over the Spanish fleet at Manila Bay in 1898
    A. guaranteed independence for the Philippines.
    B. ended the Spanish-American War.
    C. resulted in heavy American casualties.
    D. established the United States as an Asian power.

13. American actions in the Philippines from 1898 to 1902
    A. paralleled what Spain had done in Cuba.
    B. respected the principle of democracy.
    C. received united support at home.
    D. attempted to remove Spanish forces from the islands.

14. Control of the Philippines by the United States included all of the following benefits EXCEPT
    A. assuring a place among the world powers.
    B. protecting a strategic military interest in Asia.
    C. securing an economic foothold in eastern markets.
    D. providing for the triumph of democracy in the region.

ESSAY/PROBLEM QUESTIONS

15. Describe and explain the underlying and the immediate causes of the Spanish-American War. Do you think the causes justified the war? Why or why not? How did the war reflect both the self-interest and the idealism of the United States?

16. Describe and explain the arguments for imperialism and the arguments against it. Which side do you find more convincing? Why? How did the annexation of the Philippines and the events there reflect both the self-interest and the idealism of the United States?

ANSWER KEY

	Answers	Learning Objectives	Focus Points	References
1.	A	1	T1	Nash, p. 634
2.	C	1	T2, V1	Nash, pp. 637-638 and Video
3.	B	1	T3	Nash, p. 639
4.	D	1	T4	Nash, pp. 639-640
5.	D	1	T5	Nash, p. 640
6.	B	2	T6	Nash, pp. 640-641
7.	B	3	T7	Nash, pp. 643-644
8.	A	3	T8	Nash, pp. 644-647
9.	B	4	T9	Nash, pp. 646-647
10.	C	4	T10	Nash, p. 647
11.	B	2	V2	Video
12.	D	2	V3	Video
13.	A	4	V4	Video
14.	D	4	V5	Video
15.		All	All	Text and Video
16.		All	All	Text and Video

Unit Two:
A Modernizing People
1900-1945

The American people who lived during the first forty-five years of the twentieth century experienced an unusual era of triumph and tragedy. At home, the efforts of the progressives to deal with the realities of industrial capitalism highlighted the early part of the century. Then the first of two world wars enveloped the United States and ultimately changed the course of world history. The 1920s was a decade filled with transitions and tensions for people experiencing an increasingly modern America. Soon the Great Depression raised some fundamental questions about the American economic system. Out of the depths of that economic despair emerged one of the most sweeping political reform movements in American history. Franklin D. Roosevelt and the New Deal transformed the United States in ways still obvious today. Finally, World War II not only ended the economic depression, but also thrust the nation into a leadership role that it could not reject.

Lesson 8

The Progressive Impulse

LESSON ASSIGNMENTS

Review the following assignments in order to schedule your time appropriately. Pay careful attention; the titles and numbers of the textbook chapter, the telecourse guide lesson, and the video program may be different from one another.

Text: Nash et al., *The American People, Volume Two: From 1865*, Chapter 21, "The Progressives Confront Industrial Capitalism," pp. 662-683.

Reader: *Perspectives on America, Volume 2,* "Hell on Saturday Afternoon," by John F. McCormack, Jr.

Video: "The Progressive Impulse," from the series *America in Perspective.*

OVERVIEW

As the United States entered the twentieth century, it had the makings of a highly stratified society, both economically and socially. Industrialization had brought about divisions in society: divisions between the large and small manufacturers, between management and labor, between the masses of new immigrants and the old immigrants, between the "haves" and the "have-nots." Unless the trend were reversed, or at least halted, it looked as if the United States was drifting toward a condition of fixed and highly differentiated classes. One class would consist of a small but quite privileged elite, one would comprise a relatively small but increasingly significant upper middle class, and one would be made up of the masses who were relatively quite deprived. Interclass strife, which had surfaced in the 1890s, had temporarily disappeared during the Spanish-American War. However, as wartime unity faded, social tensions had the potential to rise again.

In any period of potential social unrest, whether it be at the turn of the century, the Great Depression of the 1930s, or the turbulent 1960s, the political response to the issues can be critical. During the first two decades of the twentieth century, a broad spectrum of reform-minded politicians stepped forward in an attempt to change society. They were called progressives, and they sought to take some of the rough edges off of the lives of the lower classes. They advocated political action, for they saw the government as a positive agent for change. In short, the progressives wanted to restore opportunity, in its broadest sense, through a more democratic government.

People living in the United States today take for granted that the government will be involved in their lives. Indeed, many heated discussions concern the extent of the involvement, but there nonetheless will be government involvement. Changes which occurred during the progressive era did much to shape the ongoing political debate. A passage from *The American People* helps put the significance of the progressive era in perspective:

> In many ways, progressivism was the first modern reform movement. . . . The progressives were optimistic about human nature, and they believed that change was possible. . . . they wrestled with many social questions, some of them old but fraught with new urgency in an industrialized society. What is the proper relation of government to society? In a world of large corporations, huge cities, and massive transportation systems, how much should the government regulate and control? How much responsibility does society have to care for the poor and needy? The progressives could not agree on the answers, but they struggled with the questions. (p. 665)

In their search for answers to the troubling questions of their time, progressives looked to the local, state, and national governments. In this lesson we will examine conditions which gave rise to "the progressive impulse." Then we will analyze the accomplishments and limitations of the progressives at the local and state level. We will evaluate national progressivism in the next lesson.

LEARNING OBJECTIVES

Goal—The purpose of this lesson is to increase our understanding of the motives of progressive reformers, how they attempted to deal with urban and industrial problems, and their successes and limitations at the municipal and state levels.

Objectives—Upon the completion of this lesson, you should be able to:
1. Describe who the progressive reformers were and why they took the approaches to reform that they chose.
2. Examine the major issues of the social justice progressives, and evaluate their success in achieving their goals.
3. Evaluate the status of workers and unions during the progressive era.
4. Analyze the issues addressed by the municipal reformers and the success and limitations of their efforts.
5. Assess the accomplishments and limitations of the progressives who worked for reform at the state level.

TEXT FOCUS POINTS

The following questions are designed to help you get the most from your reading. Review them before you do your reading. After completing the assignment, write responses and/or notes to reinforce what you have learned.

Text: Nash et al., *The American People*, Chapter 21, pp. 662-683.

1. How did the life of Frances Kellor illustrate the reform mentality and the actions of the progressive era?
2. Who were the muckrakers? What was their role in the progressive era?
3. How did the social justice progressives propose to deal with working women and children, education, and vice? What were the results of their reform efforts?
4. How and why did the nature of industrial work change in the early twentieth century?
5. What factors explain the gains and limitations of unions during the progressive era?
6. What were the effects of the Triangle Shirtwaist Company fire and the Ludlow Massacre?

7. Why did the Industrial Workers of the World have limited appeal in the United States?

8. Who were the municipal reformers, and what reforms did they initiate in American cities? How successful were their efforts?

9. What did Robert M. La Follette and the "Wisconsin idea" do to reform the state of Wisconsin? In general, how successful was progressive reform at the state level?

READER FOCUS POINTS

Reader: *Perspectives on America, Volume 2*, "Hell on Saturday Afternoon," by McCormack.

1. Describe the working conditions at the Triangle Shirtwaist Company in 1911.

2. What factors contributed to the likelihood of a tragic fire at the Triangle Shirtwaist Company?

3. What happened as a result of the factory fire? What did this entire episode teach us about the role of the government in regulating working conditions?

VIDEO FOCUS POINTS

The following questions are designed to help you get the most from the video segment of this lesson. Review them before you watch the video. After viewing the video segment, write responses and/or notes to reinforce what you have learned.

Video: "The Progressive Impulse"

1. What factors explain the emergence of the progressive reformers of the early twentieth century? Who were the progressive reformers and what were their beliefs?

2. How did Jane Addams and Robert La Follette further the cause of progressive reform?

3. How and why did the middle-class attitudes and actions of the progressives conflict with the attitudes and needs of those whom they were trying to help?

4. How did child labor legislation illustrate progressive reform? Why was child labor legislation resisted?

5. What were the accomplishments of the progressives at the local and state level? Who benefited from their reforms? What limited their reform efforts?

ENRICHMENT IDEAS

These activities are not required unless your instructor assigns them. They are offered as suggestions to help you learn more about the material presented in this lesson.

1. Read and analyze the "Recovering the Past" segment on pages 670-671 of *The American People.* Write a report on that segment in which you answer the questions presented in the text.
2. You are a social justice progressive in 1908. In a 750-word essay, describe the major issues about which you are concerned and explain how you propose to use the government to bring about change.

SUGGESTED READINGS

See the "Recommended Reading" listings on page 697 of the textbook if you wish to explore further the material presented in this lesson.

SUGGESTED WEB SITES

Several places in the textbook will include information marked "The History Place." This is a reference to a related web site. See the "Suggested Web Sites" at the end of the chapter of the textbook if you wish to further explore the material presented in this lesson.

PRACTICE TEST

The following items will help you evaluate your understanding of this lesson. Use the answer key at the end of the lesson to check your answers or to locate material related in each question.

MULTIPLE-CHOICE INSTRUCTIONS

Choose the single best answer. If more than one answer is required, it will be so indicated.

1. Frances Kellor was a typical progressive in all of the following respects EXCEPT that she believed that
   A. women should assume leadership roles.
   B. social ills could be corrected through government action.
   C. heredity explained social problems.
   D. issues must be thoroughly investigated.

2. Muckrakers like Lincoln Steffens, Ida Tarbell, and Robert Hunter were significant because they
   A. publicized social ills.
   B. served as reform-minded mayors.
   C. belonged to Robert M. La Follette's "brain trust."
   D. praised big business.

3. The efforts of the progressive era reformers were often limited because they frequently
   A. cooperated too closely with business leaders.
   B. had little understanding of working-class life.
   C. failed to research social problems adequately.
   D. refused to attempt to amend the Constitution.

4. One reason for the change in the nature of industrial work in the early twentieth century was the
   A. establishment of tight immigration quotas.
   B. passage of minimum wage laws for railroad workers.
   C. effort to achieve greater productivity and profits.
   D. prohibition of child labor.

5. The American Federation of Labor tended to be the most successful union during the progressive era because it
    A. promoted socialism.
    B. appealed more to traditional American values.
    C. organized only unskilled workers.
    D. recruited women workers.

6. The Ludlow Massacre resulted in a
    A. victory for the United Mine Workers.
    B. sharply critical investigation of management practices.
    C. final Indian-cavalry conflict in American history.
    D. factory fire described as the worst in American history.

7. All of the following factors limited the success of the Industrial Workers of the World EXCEPT
    A. radical image perceived by most Americans.
    B. failure to organize women and migrant workers.
    C. denunciation of Samuel Gompers and the AFL.
    D. internal squabbles and disagreements.

8. During the progressive era, those who wanted to reform the American city generally
    A. opposed the commission form of city government.
    B. feared the influence of immigrants on democratic institutions.
    C. supported working-class values.
    D. supported the same goals as the political bosses.

9. Progressive reformers at the state level
    A. promoted government efficiency but not social justice.
    B. rejected most populist ideas.
    C. opposed the use of the initiative and referendum.
    D. supported laws regulating railroad and utility companies.

10. All of the following were characteristic of work at the Triangle Shirtwaist Company in 1911 EXCEPT
    A. low safety standards.
    B. government regulation of wages and hours.
    C. management resistance to unionism.
    D. primarily female workers.

11. Exit doors of the Triangle Shirtwaist Company building had been locked because managers were concerned about workers
    A. feeling threatened by outside agitators.
    B. taking long lunch breaks.
    C. leaving work early.
    D. stealing materials.

12. As a result of the Triangle Shirtwaist Company fire,
    A. owners were convicted of murder.
    B. government more actively regulated businesses.
    C. Franklin D. Roosevelt was elected governor of New York.
    D. Congress passed social security legislation.

13. Progressive reformers tended to be
    A. rural residents.
    B. union members.
    C. recent immigrants.
    D. middleclass in background.

14. The work of Jane Addams and others at Hull House
    A. solved the housing problems of Chicago.
    B. received support from the local politicians.
    C. emerged from a detailed plan for social action.
    D. helped lay the groundwork for political reform.

15. Progressive efforts to enact child labor legislation met resistance because
    A. education was unnecessary in that era.
    B. labor shortages existed throughout that period.
    C. research showed that factory work was good for kids.
    D. many Americans thought that children should work.

16. The effectiveness of progressive reform was limited by
    A. reluctance to pay for implementation.
    B. lack of commitment by reformers.
    C. inability to succeed in amending the Constitution.
    D. ability of the free market to distribute wealth equitably.

ESSAY/PROBLEM QUESTION

17. Describe and explain the background and the issues of the progressive era.
    Why did the progressive reformers decide to approach the issues like they did?
    What changes did the progressives bring about at the city and state levels?
    What factors limited change?

ANSWER KEY

Answers	Learning Objectives	Focus Points	References
1. C	1	T1	Nash, pp. 663-664
2. A	1	T2	Nash, p. 665
3. B	2	T3, V3	Nash, pp. 665-675 and Video
4. C	3	T4	Nash, pp. 675-677
5. B	3	T5	Nash, p. 677
6. B	3	T6	Nash, p. 679
7. B	3	T7	Nash, pp. 679-680
8. B	4	T8	Nash, pp. 680-682
9. D	5	T9	Nash, pp. 682-683
10. B	3	R1	Reader
11. D	3	R2	Reader
12. B	3	R3	Reader
13. D	1	V1	Video
14. D	4	V2	Video
15. D	2	V4	Video
16. A	4, 5	V5	Video
17.	All	All	Text, Reader, and Video

Lesson 9

The Progressive Presidents

LESSON ASSIGNMENTS

Review the following assignments in order to schedule your time appropriately. Pay careful attention; the titles and numbers of the textbook chapter, the telecourse guide lesson, and the video program may be different from one another.

Text: Nash et al., *The American People, Volume Two: From 1865,*
        Chapter 21, "The Progressives Confront Industrial Capitalism,"
        pp. 683-698.

Reader: *Perspectives on America, Volume 2,* "Who Put the Borax in Dr. Wiley's Butter?," by Gerald H. Carson.

Video: "The Progressive Presidents,"
        from the series *America in Perspective.*

OVERVIEW

Although progressives at the local and state levels made significant contributions toward a better America, their effect was obviously limited. The United States was more than ever a nation with issues which went well beyond the reach of local and state governments. Between 1901 and 1917, presidents and congressional representatives dealt with such concerns as business regulation, conservation, consumer protection, and tax reform—all issues of relevance to Americans living today.

When President William McKinley was assassinated in September 1901, the man Marcus Hanna called "that damned cowboy" assumed the presidency of the United States. Upon taking the presidential oath, Theodore Roosevelt promised to continue, "absolutely unbroken," the policies of his predecessor. However, long before he left office in 1909, Roosevelt had ushered in a new era in presidential politics.

Theodore Roosevelt (TR) came to the presidency with a sense of the pressing economic and social issues which had developed in industrial America. More significantly, he was the first president since the Civil War who was willing and able to provide national leadership in addressing those issues. TR liked having the power of the presidency, and he always held a strong conviction that he could use that power in the interests of the public. His actions as president have led several observers to call him the first modern president and the best publicity man progressivism ever had. Despite his rambunctious appearance, he did not go to extremes. Rather, he maintained a moderate but meaningful course of reform. He impressed upon the right wing of his party that they had to give a little if they hoped to preserve the middle ground. He demonstrated to the leftists of the era that changes could be made through the existing political process.

When Roosevelt's hand-picked successor, William Howard Taft, won the 1908 presidential election, TR expected that his policies and programs would continue. But just as Roosevelt was no McKinley, Taft would not be another Roosevelt. By 1910, many leading progressives and Taft were nearing a complete break. Even Taft's progressive acts—his aid in strengthening some railroad regulation, his prosecution of more trusts than Roosevelt, and his support for the income tax amendment—were not enough to satisfy the reformers. Indeed, President Taft, who never appeared comfortable as president and lacked the charisma of his predecessor, seemed to be reluctantly tagging along rather than leading the country.

Taft's difficulties were enhanced when former president Theodore Roosevelt challenged him for the Republican nomination for president in 1912. Taft received the nomination, but TR's decision to bolt the Republican party and run as a third-party candidate practically assured the Democrat Woodrow Wilson of election.

There is no doubt that the results of the 1912 election indicated that the voters were overwhelmingly progressive in temperament. Those voting for Wilson or Roosevelt were clearly voting for more reform. In addition, the Socialist candidate Eugene Debs, who called for nationalization of the nation's major industries, received some 900,000 votes in the election. Wilson, therefore, was entering the presidency with a mandate for more progressive reform. With Democratic majorities in both houses of Congress and likely support coming from progressive Republicans, Wilson was ready to push the national progressive agenda forward.

Wilson brought to the presidency his strength of intellect and his commitment. As one commentator has said, "if under [Theodore] Roosevelt social reform had taken on all the excitement of a circus, under Wilson it acquired the dedication of a sunrise service." President Wilson's inaugural address was a moving statement of progressivism, as he summoned "all honest men, all patriotic, and all forward-looking men" to his side to correct the evils of the country. During his first term, he marshaled enough support to bring about significant changes in tariff, banking, antitrust, and regulatory legislation. But then World War I diverted almost everyone's attention to foreign affairs. The effects of the war crushed Wilson politically and helped lead to the end of the progressive era.

While recognizing the limitations of the progressives, particularly in the area of minority rights, they did play an important role in American political history. They helped purge society of some of its worst abuses. They opened up avenues for more direct popular participation in the political process. They had taken some of the rough edges off of industrial America. Much still needed to be done, but at least they made a moderate beginning.

LEARNING OBJECTIVES

Goal—The purpose of this lesson is to increase our understanding of the lasting significance of national progressive reform, particularly as expressed during the presidencies of Theodore Roosevelt and Woodrow Wilson.

Objectives—Upon completion of this lesson, you should be able to:
1. Assess the presidency of Theodore Roosevelt both in the context of the progressive era and its long-term significance.
2. Describe and explain the successes and the shortcomings of the Taft presidency.
3. Analyze the presidential election of 1912 in the context of the progressive era.
4. Assess the presidency of Woodrow Wilson both in the context of the progressive era and its long-term significance.
5. Evaluate the changes brought about during the national progressive era, what limited those changes, and the connection between the progressives and later reformers.

TEXT FOCUS POINTS

The following questions are designed to help you get the most from your reading. Review them before you do your reading. After completing the assignment, write responses and/or notes to reinforce what you have learned.

Text: Nash et. al., *The American People*, Chapter 21, pp. 683-698.

1. How did President Theodore Roosevelt deal with trusts and union labor? What were the results of his actions?
2. In what ways were the Meat Inspection Act and the Pure Food and Drug Act typical of national progressive reform?
3. Describe the views of Gifford Pinchot, John Muir, and Theodore Roosevelt regarding conservation. What resulted from the actions taken by these three individuals in the area of conservation?
4. Why was progressivism largely "for whites only"? How did the NAACP respond to conditions during this era?
5. What were the accomplishments and limitations of the Taft presidency?
6. What was the significance of the 1912 presidential election?
7. What were the accomplishments and limitations of the Wilson presidency, particularly in the areas of tax reform, banking, corporate regulation, and social reform?
8. How did the progressive presidents, especially Theodore Roosevelt and Woodrow Wilson, change the presidency and the nature of the role of the federal government?

READER FOCUS POINTS

Reader: *Perspectives on America, Volume 2,* "Who Put the Borax in Dr. Wiley's Butter?," by Carson.

1. Why was a pure food and drugs law needed in late nineteenth and early twentieth century America?
2. Why was there so much opposition to a pure food and drugs law? What factors finally led to the enactment of the law?
3. What were the effects of the pure food and drugs laws, both for the consumers and the manufacturers? Why was the legislation typical of progressive reform?

VIDEO FOCUS POINTS

The following focus points are designed to help you get the most from the video segment of this lesson. Review them, then watch the video. You may want to write notes to reinforce what you have learned.

Video: "The Progressive Presidents"

1. Why was federal action necessary in order to deal effectively with economic and social problems in the early part of the twentieth century?
2. How and why did Theodore Roosevelt help change the role of the president and the federal government in general regarding business regulation, labor relations, consumer protection, and the environment?
3. Why did the progressives use the process of amending the Constitution? What amendments were enacted?
4. Why do some consider the actions of the progressives to be "conservative"? What limited progressivism?
5. How are the progressives linked to later reform eras? What does the entire progressive era teach us about bringing about change in America?

ENRICHMENT IDEAS

These activities are not required unless your instructor assigns them. They are offered as suggestions to help you learn more about the material presented in this lesson.

1. Read *The Jungle* by Upton Sinclair and then write a critical analysis of it.
2. You are a progressive in the early twentieth century. In a well-reasoned 750-word essay, identify three major domestic issues facing the nation and describe what you propose to do about them through national political action.

SUGGESTED READINGS

See the "Recommended Reading" listings on page 697 of the text if you wish to explore further the material presented in this lesson.

SUGGESTED WEB SITES

Several places in the textbook will include information marked "The History Place." This is a reference to a related web site. See the "Suggested Web Sites" at the end of the chapter of the textbook if you wish to further explore the material presented in this lesson.

PRACTICE TEST

The following items will help you evaluate your understanding of this lesson. Use the answer key at the end of the lesson to check your answers or to locate material related in each question.

MULTIPLE-CHOICE INSTRUCTIONS

Choose the single best answer. If more than one answer is required, it will be so indicated.

1. In the anthracite coal strike of 1902, Theodore Roosevelt
    A. showed that he would follow the policies of McKinley.
    B. supported use of the strike to achieve the workers' goals.
    C. assumed the role of a mediator.
    D. created public sympathy for the mine owners.

2. The Meat Inspection and Pure Food and Drug Acts represent typical progressive reform measures since they
    A. benefited both business and the consumer.
    B. achieved effectiveness only at the state level.
    C. seemed to have little effect on business operations.
    D. passed Congress but were vetoed by the president.

3. As a result of the efforts of Gifford Pinchot, John Muir, and Theodore Roosevelt,
    A. private developers received access to public lands.
    B. public lands were protected from private exploitation.
    C. establishment of the Environmental Protection Agency occurred.
    D. trees were planted by the Civilian Conservation Corps.

4. Most progressive leaders ignored the problems of blacks because they were
   A. more interested in foreign affairs.
   C. usually insensitive to the social ills of the era.
   D. still thinking in sterotypical racial terms.

5. President Taft created a split in the Republican party over his actions regarding
   A. regulation of foods and drugs.
   B. opposition to municipal reform.
   C. curbing of Speaker Cannon's powers.
   D. tariff and conservation issues.

6. The results of the presidential election of 1912 indicated that voters wanted
   A. socialist policies enacted.
   B. corporate power unchallenged by government.
   C. additional progressive reforms implemented.
   D. federal income tax proposals dropped.

7. Support for the establishment of a Federal Trade Commission demonstrated President Wilson's interest in
   A. undermining the free-enterprise system.
   B. maintaining unregulated freedom of competition.
   C. supporting Theodore Roosevelt's New Nationalism philosophy.
   D. demonstrating sympathy for labor unions.

8. During their presidencies, Theodore Roosevelt and Woodrow Wilson
   A. satisfied most of the demands of the political radicals.
   B. reduced the regulatory power of the federal government.
   C. emphasized social justice more than economic regulation.
   D. increased the power of the executive branch of government.

9. A pure food and drugs law was needed in late nineteenth and early twentieth century America because
   A. prices for food and drugs were too high.
   B. processed food was heavily laced with untested chemicals.
   C. manufacturers were advocating government help.
   D. farmers were demanding price supports.

10. Those opposed to the passage of a pure food and drugs law in the early twentieth century included all of the following EXCEPT
    A. big business lobbyists.
    B. chemical manufacturers.
    C. magazines like *Leslie's Weekly*.
    D. labor unions.

11. Court decisions in the late nineteenth century
    A. upheld the federal income tax.
    B. assured that monopolies would not exist.
    C. maintained that railroads must give rebates to farmers.
    D. impeded state regulation of large businesses.

12. During the progressive era, the Constitution was amended to do all of the following EXCEPT provide for
    A. collection of an income tax.
    B. direct election of senators.
    C. women's suffrage.
    D. abolition of poll taxes.

13. All of the following ingredients were associated with progressive efforts to change America EXCEPT
    A. effective organization.
    B. outspoken leadership.
    C. militant revolutionary activity.
    D. willingness to work within the system.

ESSAY/PROBLEM QUESTIONS

14. Describe and explain how Presidents Theodore Roosevelt and Woodrow Wilson handled the major domestic issues of their presidencies. In your answer, be sure to consider their successes and limitations and their effect on the role of the president.

15. Describe and explain the major changes brought about by progressives at the local, state, and national levels. What limited those changes? What is the legacy of the progressive era?

ANSWER KEY

Answers	Learning Objectives	Focus Points	References
1. C	1	T1, V2	Nash, p. 685 and Video
2. A	1	T2, R3	Nash, pp. 686-687 and Reader
3. B	1	T3	Nash, pp. 687-688
4. D	5	T4, V4	Nash, pp. 688-689 and Video
5. D	2	T5	Nash, p. 690
6. C	3	T6	Nash, pp. 690-693
7. C	4	T7	Nash, p. 695
8. D	5	T8	Nash, p. 696
9. B	5	R1	Reader
10. D	5	R2	Reader
11. D	1	V1	Video
12. D	5	V3	Video
13. C	5	V5	Video
14.	All	All	Text, Reader, and Video
15.	All	All	Text, Reader, and Video

Lesson 10

The Big Stick

LESSON ASSIGNMENTS

Review the following assignments in order to schedule your time appropriately. Pay careful attention; the titles and numbers of the textbook chapter, the telecourse guide lesson, and the video program may be different from one another.

Text: Nash et al., *The American People, Volume Two: From 1865,* Chapter 20, "Becoming a World Power," pp. 644-661; and Chapter 22, "The Great War," pp. 707-709.

Video: "The Big Stick," from the series *America in Perspective.*

OVERVIEW

Although the United States is only one of many nations on the continents of North and South America, the term "America" is often used interchangeably with "United States." That says much about the perception of the United States as the major nation in the Americas. That perception may not have begun with the Spanish-American War, but it was certainly reinforced by the results of that war and the actions taken shortly thereafter. At the beginning of this century, the United States wielded a "big stick" in Latin America, intervening for strategic, economic, and political reasons. However, one's view of the "big stick" may well depend on whether one is on the delivering or receiving end of it!

Recall that at the end of the nineteenth century, the United States had extended its empire to include the Philippines, Guam, Hawaii, and Puerto Rico. This had pleased the imperialists, who believed that the United States was destined to spread democracy, expand its markets, flex its muscles, and in brief, "civilize" various parts of the world.

By 1901, with the assassination of President William McKinley and the assumption of the presidency by Theodore Roosevelt, the United States was led by a man who was not only comfortable with the office but also with the United States as a world power. TR has been called the first modern president both because he grasped the realities of big business on the domestic scene and because he understood the realities of power politics on the international scene. His world views very much coincided with the imperialists, and he was willing to carry out U.S. diplomacy with gusto.

Roosevelt supposedly adopted as his pet proverb the saying, "Speak softly and carry a big stick." He believed that the military preparedness and presence of the United States would assure that the United States could wield a "big stick" to maintain his version of a balance of power. Outside of the western hemisphere, that meant that Roosevelt would work with the other major world powers to preserve order. Within the western hemisphere, using the "big stick" meant direct U.S. intervention.

During Roosevelt's presidency, the United States intervened throughout the Caribbean region, but TR's actions regarding Panama were particularly illustrative of his view of the role the United States must play in the area. Gaining the rights to build a canal through Panama shaped many of the subsequent U.S. policies in the region. In 1904, Roosevelt gave expression to a basic concept behind these policies when he announced what became known as the Roosevelt Corollary to the Monroe Doctrine:

> If a nation shows that it knows how to act with reasonable efficiency and decency in social and political matters, if it keeps order and pays its obligations, it need fear no interference from the United States. Chronic wrong-doing, or an impotence which results in a general loosening of the ties of civilized society . . . may force the United States . . . to the exercise of an international police power.

TR's successor, William Howard Taft, did not appear to share Roosevelt's enthusiasm for power politics. Nevertheless, Taft continued to use U.S. troops to intervene, and he intensified the economic expansion by the United States in the area. Called "dollar diplomacy," the idea was to try wherever possible to create investment opportunities for American dollars. Since investors wanted stability, the dollars sometimes became reasons for further military intervention. In addition, U.S. corporations which established themselves in the region became powerful economically and politically, and eventually became the object of much resentment.

When Woodrow Wilson came to the presidency in 1913, he rejected dollar diplomacy in favor of what he termed "human rights, national integrity, and opportunity." He believed that the mission of the United States in the world was to be the bearer of justice, morality, and democracy—not the big stick. Wilson preached that negotiation, disarmament, and international fair play were the ways to a peaceful and prosperous world. Despite his lofty idealism, Wilson found himself authorizing intervention in Latin America for basically the same reasons as his predecessors, and with many of the same results.

When President Wilson withdrew American troops from Mexico in early 1917, his missionary diplomacy was about to embark on an even greater challenge "to make the world safe for democracy." Perhaps the approaching involvement in a world war was an inescapable result of the place the United States occupied in the world by 1917. In less than two decades, the United States had fought the Spanish-American War and made a decision for empire. Establishing that empire had proven costly in terms of death, money, and ill will. The benefits of it were measured in terms of trade expansion and the prestige of world power status. In Latin America, the United States had secured territory, a valuable naval base in Cuba, and the Panama Canal. Intervening militarily, economically, and politically in almost every country in the region, the United States had established a pattern that it would follow for the rest of the century.

LEARNING OBJECTIVES

Goal—The purpose of this lesson is to increase our understanding of U.S. foreign policy in the early part of the twentieth century and how that policy affects the nation today.

Objectives—Upon completion of this lesson, you should be able to:
1. Describe and explain President Theodore Roosevelt's world view and the actions he took to implement his diplomacy.
2. Analyze the causes and consequences of "dollar diplomacy."
3. Compare and contrast President Woodrow Wilson's world view and Latin American diplomacy with the views and diplomacy of Presidents Theodore Roosevelt and William Howard Taft.
4. Assess both the short-term and long-term consequences of U.S. "big stick" diplomacy during this era.

TEXT FOCUS POINTS

The following questions are designed to help you get the most from your reading. Review them before you do your reading. After completing the assignment, write responses and/or notes to reinforce what you have learned.

Text: Nash et al., *The American People,* Chapter 20, pp. 644-661; and Chapter 22, pp. 707-709.

1. How did Theodore Roosevelt's personality and personal principles extend to national foreign policies? How did Roosevelt perceive the function of power and "civilized nations" in the world?
2. How and why did the United States acquire rights to the Panama Canal? What was the significance of this?
3. What was the significance of Roosevelt's Corollary to the Monroe Doctrine? How and why did the United States intervene in Cuba and the Dominican Republic?
4. Why did the United States pursue an Open Door policy regarding China? What complicated American relations with the Chinese?
5. Why did Theodore Roosevelt mediate the Russo-Japanese War? What effects did this have on later United States-Japanese relations?
6. What were President Roosevelt's views and policies regarding foreign relations with European nations?
7. How did President Woodrow Wilson's Latin American diplomacy differ from that of Presidents Roosevelt and Taft? What were the effects of Wilson's intervention in Mexico?

VIDEO FOCUS POINTS

The following questions are designed to help you get the most from the video segment of this lesson. Review them before you watch the video. After viewing the video segment, write responses and/or notes to reinforce what you have learned.

Video: "The Big Stick"

1. Compare and contrast the major points of emphasis of American foreign policy under Presidents Theodore Roosevelt, William Howard Taft, and Woodrow Wilson. How different were the results of their policies?
2. How did the United States acquire the Panama Canal? How important was this to American policy in the region? How did Latin Americans react to acquisition of the Panama Canal by the United States?
3. What role did Philippe Bunau-Varilla play in the acquisition of the Panama Canal by the United States?
4. Why was the intervention of the United States in Latin America supported? Why was intervention opposed?
5. What were the short-term and the long-term consequences of intervention in Latin America by the United States?

ENRICHMENT IDEAS

These activities are not required unless your instructor assigns them. They are offered as suggestions to help you learn more about the material presented in this lesson.

1. Read and analyze the "Recovering the Past" segment on pages 652-653 of *The American People*. Then check newspapers or news magazines for political cartoons relating to recent American foreign policy. Submit copies of two such cartoons, citing the sources and dates. Include with the cartoons a brief analysis of the meaning of the cartoons and the point of view of the cartoonist.
2. Research and analyze the Panama Canal Treaties of 1978. Then write a well-developed 750-word essay describing the terms of those treaties and explaining how the manner in which the United States originally acquired the canal in 1903 may have affected the 1978 treaties. Also, state and defend your own personal

opinion on the relinquishment of the Panama Canal by the United States at the end of this century.

SUGGESTED READINGS

See the "Recommended Reading" listings on page 660 of the text if you wish to explore further the material presented in this lesson.

SUGGESTED WEB SITES

Several places in the textbook will include information marked "The History Place." These are references to related web sites. See the "Suggested Web Sites" at the end of the chapters in the textbook if you wish to further explore the material presented in this lesson.

PRACTICE TEST

The following items will help you evaluate your understanding of this lesson. Use the answer key at the end of the lesson to check your answers or to locate material related in each question.

MULTIPLE-CHOICE INSTRUCTIONS

Choose the single best answer. If more than one answer is required, it will be so indicated.

1. According to Theodore Roosevelt, American foreign policy should be based on the concept that
   A. all nations should enjoy the same rights.
   B. larger nations should carefully protect smaller nations.
   C. struggle exists between nations as between individuals.
   D. "white man's burden" contradicted America's democratic traditions.

2. In acquiring the right to build a canal across Panama, the United States
   A. respected the sensibilities of the Colombians.
   B. gained the respect and admiration of other Latin American countries.
   C. opposed Panamanian nationalists who wanted independence.
   D. facilitated a Panamanian revolution against Colombia.

3. The Roosevelt Corollary to the Monroe Doctrine was announced to justify American
   A. "good neighbor" policy with Latin America.
   B. intervention in the Dominican Republic.
   C. economic assistance program for the Caribbean.
   D. acquisition of the Panama canal.

4. One purpose of the Open Door policy was to
   A. preserve the balance of power by protecting Chinese territorial integrity.
   B. block a Chinese invasion of Japan.
   C. establish a monopoly for American business interests.
   D. encourage Chinese immigration to the United States.

5. President Theodore Roosevelt mediated a settlement in the Russo-Japanese War in 1905 in order to
   A. pay back the Russians for their help in the Philippines.
   B. help the Japanese establish dominance in Asia.
   C. form a military alliance with Japan.
   D. maintain the balance of power in the Far East.

6. During the Theodore Roosevelt administration, American foreign policy toward Europe stressed
   A. close relationship with the British.
   B. military alliance against the Germans.
   C. belief that Asia was more important to world peace than Europe.
   D. German rather than French control of Morocco.

7. The major difference between the Latin American policy of Woodrow Wilson and that of Presidents Theodore Roosevelt and Taft was that Wilson
   A. refused to authorize intervention.
   B. recognized Central American governments no matter how they came to power.
   C. used rhetoric which emphasized idealistic aims.
   D. achieved revered stature in Mexico.

8. Philippe Bunau-Varilla played all of the following roles in the acquisition of the Panama Canal by the United States EXCEPT
   A. conspirator.
   B. revolutionary.
   C. lobbyist.
   D. dictator.

9. Those who opposed U.S. intervention in Latin America argued that the
   A. practice contradicted the democratic spirit.
   B. Panama Canal was too expensive to build.
   C. refugees from the area would take away American jobs.
   D. Roosevelt Corollary was unconstitutional.

10. In the video program, Professor Robert Beisner maintained that one of the long-term consequences of U.S. intervention in Latin America during the early part of the twentieth century was
    A. greater respect for European assistance in the area.
    B. increased achievement of equal economic opportunity.
    C. more dependence of Latin American countries on the United States.
    D. diminished immigration from the area.

ESSAY/PROBLEM QUESTIONS

11. How and why did the United States apply the "big stick" policy in Latin America during the period 1901-1917? What were the results of this policy?

12. Describe and explain how and why the United States acquired the Panama Canal in 1903. What were the effects of the Canal on U.S. policy in the region? State and defend your personal opinion on the wisdom of the Panama Canal treaties in which the United States relinquished the canal to Panama at the end of the century.

ANSWER KEY

Answers	Learning Objectives	Focus Points	References
1. C	1	T1	Nash, p. 648
2. D	1	T2, V2	Nash, pp. 650-651 and Video
3. B	1	T3	Nash, pp. 654-655
4. A	1	T4	Nash, pp. 655-656
5. D	1	T5	Nash, pp. 656-657
6. A	1	T6	Nash, pp. 658-659
7. C	3	T7, V1	Nash, pp. 707-709 and Video
8. D	1	V3	Video
9. A	4	V4	Video
10. C	4	V5	Video
11.	All	All	Text and Video
12.	All	All	Text and Video

Lesson 11

The Great War

LESSON ASSIGNMENTS

Review the following assignments in order to schedule your time appropriately. Pay careful attention; the titles and numbers of the textbook chapter, the telecourse guide lesson, and the video program may be different from one another.

Text: Nash et al., *The American People, Volume Two: From 1865,* Chapter 22, "The Great War," pp. 700-729.

Reader: *Perspectives on America, Volume 2,* "1918," by John Lukacs.

Video: "The Great War," from the series *America in Perspective.*

OVERVIEW

When President Woodrow Wilson withdrew U.S. forces from Mexico in 1917, he was not abandoning his democratic mission. Rather, it was now time "to make the world safe for democracy." World War I became the "Great War," a "war to end all wars"—in short, it became a crusade which affected millions of people and altered the course of world history. When it was over, disillusionment prevailed. Why had we fought? What were the costs and benefits? What did we learn as a people and a nation?

When war broke out in Europe late in the summer of 1914, President Wilson proclaimed that the United States would remain neutral. This traditional policy made sense at the time, for a neutral nation could trade with both sides in the war and did not have to commit troops to the conflict. To most Americans, the war was "over there," and they hoped it would stay that way.

Both the Allies and the Central Powers violated American neutrality, but German violations led to the direct loss of American lives. German unrestricted submarine warfare, fears of German militarism, and revelation of a proposed

German alliance with Mexico against the United States caused the United States to side with the Allies. Strong economic and cultural ties to the Allies also influenced the American decision to enter the war in the spring of 1917.

The American entrance into the world war necessitated a mobilization of the nation's resources—human as well as material. "It is not an army we must train for war," Wilson said, "it is a nation." To accomplish this training, Congress delegated to the president extensive power to enforce wartime legislation and to reorganize the government and the nation's resources for greater efficiency. Not since the Civil War had the whole nation been so affected by such an extensive effort.

American forces may have entered the war late, but they did make a difference. Finally, at the eleventh hour of the eleventh day of the eleventh month—November 11, 1918, the Germans signed an armistice that ended the fighting. They maintained that the armistice was based on President Wilson's Fourteen Points.

Wilson had announced these idealistic objectives for the war—or, more significantly, for the peace following it—in January 1918. Wilson was not able to incorporate all of his Fourteen Points into the Treaty of Versailles, but he did get world leaders to agree to create a League of Nations. Tragically for Wilson, he failed to achieve Senate ratification of the Treaty of Versailles, and therefore, the United States never joined the League.

Millions of Americans experienced a second world war in their lifetime largely because of the unsatisfactory settlement of World War I. Most historians agree that the "Great War" had caused such hardship that the Treaty of Versailles was unable to repair the damage. In fact, it may have exacerbated underlying tensions and created new dangers. At war's end, President Wilson and the United States appeared to stand at the pinnacle of world power. Neither Wilson nor the United States was able to take full advantage of this favorable position. Wilson, the United States, and the world were worse off as a result.

LEARNING OBJECTIVES

Goal—The purpose of this lesson is to increase our understanding of the causes of World War I, the reasons the United States entered the war, and the effects of the war on the American people and nation.

Objectives—Upon completion of this lesson, you should be able to:
1. Analyze the causes of World War I and the American response to that war before the United States entered it.
2. Describe and explain why the United States entered World War I and how the government prepared the nation to fight once that decision was made.
3. Describe the effects of the military experience on the American soldiers and the significance of the American contribution to the war effort.
4. Analyze the political, economic, and social effects of the war on the American home front.
5. Assess the position of the United States in the world in 1918, President Wilson's role in the peacemaking process, and why the U.S. Senate rejected the Treaty of Versailles.

TEXT FOCUS POINTS

The following questions are designed to help you get the most from your reading. Review them before you do your reading. After completing the assignment, write responses and/or notes to reinforce what you have learned.

Text: Nash et al., *The American People*, Chapter 22, pp. 700-729.

1. What were the causes of the European war?
2. How did the American people react to news of the European war? Why did the United States proclaim neutrality? How was that neutrality violated?
3. What factors eventually brought the United States into the war on the Allied side?
4. How did the government rally public support for the war? How were those who were opposed to the war treated?
5. How did the United States recruit people for the military service? What were some common characteristics of the troops? What role did women play in the war?

6. How were black soldiers treated in the American military? How were American soldiers assigned to fighting units? How important were American soldiers in bringing about Allied victory?

7. How did the government finance the war? How did the role of government change during wartime? What effects did the war have on workers and the work force?

8. In what ways did World War I bring about the climax of the progressive era?

9. What purposes were served by President Wilson's Fourteen Points? What role did Wilson play at the Paris Peace Conference?

10. Why did the United States reject membership in the League of Nations? What were the effects of that decision?

READER FOCUS POINTS

Reader: *Perspectives on America, Volume 2*, "1918," by Lukacs.

1. Why was the year 1918 a turning point for the United States in respect to world affairs?

2. How does the author compare and contrast the U.S. position in the world in 1918 with that of 1945?

VIDEO FOCUS POINTS

The following questions are designed to help you get the most from the video segment of this lesson. Review them before you watch the video. After viewing the video segment, write responses and/or notes to reinforce what you have learned.

Video: "The Great War"

1. Why did war break out in Europe in 1914? Why did the United States enter the war in 1917?

2. What were the positive and negative aspects of mobilizing the American people to participate in World War I?

3. How did the realities of fighting in World War I clash with romantic notions of war? In what ways did the United States contribute to the Allied victory?

4. Why did the U.S. Senate fail to ratify the Treaty of Versailles and join the League of Nations?

5. What were the consequences of World War I in relation to U.S. history? How did that war affect world history?

ENRICHMENT IDEAS

These activities are not required unless your instructor assigns them. They are offered as suggestions to help you learn more about the material presented in this lesson.

1. Read the novel *All Quiet on the Western Front* by Erich Maria Remarque or the novel *Farewell to Arms* by Ernest Hemingway and then write a critical analysis of the book that you have read.
2. You are a U.S. Senator in 1919-1920. Write a 750-word position paper in which you defend your vote for or against the ratification of the Treaty of Versailles.
3. Read and analyze the "Recovering the Past" segment on pages 714-715 of *The American People*. Write a report on that segment in which you answer the questions presented in the text.
4. Read the article "I Was Arrested, Of Course . . ." in *Perspectives on America, Volume 2*. Then write a 750-word essay in which you summarize the article and analyze what it says about Alice Paul and the women's suffrage movement.

SUGGESTED READINGS

See the "Recommended Reading" listings on page 729 of the text if you wish to explore further the material presented in this lesson.

SUGGESTED WEB SITES

Several places in the textbook will include information marked "The History Place." This is a reference to a related web site. See the "Suggested Web Sites" at the end of the chapter of the textbook if you wish to further explore the material presented in this lesson.

PRACTICE TEST

The following items will help you evaluate your understanding of this lesson. Use the answer key at the end of the lesson to check your answers or to locate material related in each question.

MULTIPLE-CHOICE INSTRUCTIONS

Choose the single best answer. If more than one answer is required, it will be so indicated.

1. The assassination of Archduke Ferdinand in 1914 led to a war in Europe because
   A. anarchists were in control of Austria.
   B. military, economic, and political rivalries were strong.
   C. his assassin was a German nationalist.
   D. communism dominated European politics.

2. In 1914, the general American reaction to the outbreak of war in Europe was
   A. renewal of old hostilities with England.
   B. a strong desire to fight Germany.
   C. relief that the United States was uninvolved.
   D. complete neutrality of mind and action.

3. A shift in American public opinion in favor of an Allied victory in World War I occurred when
   A. German submarine warfare killed Americans.
   B. France joined forces with England.
   C. Wilson was reelected in 1916.
   D. Austria attacked Serbia.

4. As a result of the actions of the Committee on Public Information, headed by George Creel,
   A. anti-German activities became quite common.
   B. immigration quotas were lifted.
   C. government controls on the economy were diminished.
   D. the Sedition Act was declared unconstitutional.

5. The selective service system implemented by the Wilson administration
   A. failed to provide sufficient recruits for the military efforts in Europe.
   B. originated through the leadership of Theodore Roosevelt.
   C. allowed some young men to avoid military service.
   D. resulted in massive riots against the draft.

6. During World War I, the black soldier was
   A. proven to be superior to the white soldier.
   B. condemned by W. E. B. Du Bois for participating in the war.
   C. seldom treated equally by white American soldiers.
   D. prohibited from fighting under French commanders.

7. In mobilizing the American economy during World War I, the Wilson administration
   A. issued rationing stamps to limit food consumption.
   B. failed to recognize the importance of women as consumers.
   C. quickly increased the construction of battleships.
   D. used the power of the government to control scarce materials.

8. During World War I, social justice progressives in the United States
   A. achieved no government support for their policies.
   B. endorsed all aspects of the Wilson war policies.
   C. failed to restrict alcohol consumption and prostitution near military bases.
   D. criticized the government's restriction on freedom of speech.

9. In comparison with the European leaders at the Paris Peace Conference, President Wilson can be characterized as more
   A. idealistic in his proposals.
   B. hostile toward Germany.
   C. opposed to self-determination.
   D. unpopular with ordinary Europeans.

10. The U.S. Senate rejected the Treaty of Versailles and the League of Nations for all of the following reasons EXCEPT
    A. partisan politics.
    B. feuding between Wilson and Lodge.
    C. failure to compromise.
    D. Lodge's failing health.

11. The year 1918 was a turning point for the United States in world affairs for all of the following reasons EXCEPT
    A. American troops had helped win the war for the Allies.
    B. Europeans looked upon the United States with admiration and gratitude.
    C. European intellectuals hoped that President Wilson's idealism would shape the peace settlement.
    D. American membership in the League of Nations was assured.

12. In 1918, unlike 1945, the United States and its allies
    A. lost the peace almost immediately afterward.
    B. showed great compassion to their former enemies.
    C. shared their victory with the Soviet Union.
    D. displayed a sense of despair.

13. For American soldiers fighting in World War I, romantic notions regarding war were dispelled by the
    A. impersonal nature of modern warfare.
    B. anti-American protests in France.
    C. lack of any significant action.
    D. harshness of basic training.

14. After World War I, the United States was characterized by all of the following conditions EXCEPT
    A. strong international economic power.
    B. determination to live up to Wilson's idealistic principles.
    C. status as the world's leading creditor nation.
    D. rejection of political power on the world stage.

ESSAY/PROBLEM QUESTIONS

15. Describe and explain why the United States proclaimed neutrality at the beginning of World War I, how that neutrality was violated, and why the United States entered the war on the side of the Allies.

16. Describe and explain the mixed legacy of World War I both in terms of American domestic life and the role of the United States in international affairs.

ANSWER KEY

	Answers	Learning Objectives	Focus Points	References
1.	B	1	T1, V1	Nash, pp. 702-703 and Video
2.	C	1	T2	Nash, p. 703
3.	A	2	T3	Nash, p. 706
4.	A	2	T4, V2	Nash, pp. 710-712 and Video
5.	C	2	T5	Nash, p. 713
6.	C	3	T6	Nash, pp. 716-717
7.	D	4	T7	Nash, pp. 720-721
8.	D	4	T8	Nash, p. 723
9.	A	5	T9	Nash, p. 725
10.	D	5	T10, V4	Nash, pp. 727-728 and Video
11.	D	5	R1	Reader
12.	A	5	R2	Reader
13.	A	3	V3	Video
14.	B	5	V5	Video
15.		All	All	Text, Reader, and Video
16.		All	All	Text, Reader, and Video

Lesson 12

Transitions and Tensions: The 1920s

LESSON ASSIGNMENTS

Review the following assignments in order to schedule your time appropriately. Pay careful attention; the titles and numbers of the textbook chapter, the telecourse guide lesson, and the video program may be different from one another.

Text: Nash et al., *The American People, Volume Two: From 1865*, Chapter 23, "Affluence and Anxiety," pp. 730-766.

Video: "Transitions and Tensions: The 1920s," from the series *America in Perspective*.

OVERVIEW

It is easy to see why the decade of the 1920s has fascinated historians. On the one hand, the era conjures up images of fun and liberation, of sports heroes and flapper girls dancing the Charleston. On the other hand, the twenties projects visions of rigidity and narrowness, of social controls like prohibition and the specter of Ku Klux Klan marches. In actuality, the 1920s was both liberating and reactionary.

Economically, the period from 1921 to 1929 was characterized by industrial growth and increased productivity. Corporate managers initiated a system of "welfare capitalism" to improve the work environment. Workers became even more productive, and new industries emerged or expanded to unprecedented levels. Americans heard the first commercial radio broadcast in 1920, and by 1929, forty percent of their homes had radios. Other home appliances became more common, as advertisers encouraged homemakers to buy all the modern conveniences. In the 1920s, the automobile began to have tremendous effects on both American economic and social life. Meanwhile, the stock market took off to unprecedented heights.

Per capita income rose, although the rich were getting richer much faster than the lower and middle classes were improving their standard of living. Most farmers did not share in the apparent prosperity, and minority groups still were at the bottom of the income charts. However, the inherent problems of this relatively poor distribution of income did not become clear until the Great Crash and Depression starting in 1929.

Political developments during the 1920s were often obscured by the economic trends. The Republican presidents of the decade are more remembered for their inaction rather than their leadership. Warren Harding's administration was marked by corruption, but the president's death in 1923 allowed him to escape personal responsibility. Calvin Coolidge, who followed Harding, deliberately converted his administration into a "businessman's government." He gave business its head, seeing that the government intervened as little as possible. Coolidge, wrote Irving Stone, "aspired to become the least president the country ever had; he attained his desire."

In essence, therefore, the political response to the issues of the 1920s was to grant the wishes of the corporate managers. The essential political question of the 1920s was whether the business interest, given full support by a cooperative government, would conduct itself in the best interests of the American people. By the time President Herbert Hoover had finished his term, the Great Depression of the 1930s answered that question for that generation of Americans.

American society seemed to be changing quickly during the 1920s. The "flapper girl," who bobbed her hair, wore short skirts, a tight felt hat, two strings of beads around her neck, bangles on her wrists, and danced the Charleston, symbolized the "new woman." African Americans listened to a new and more radical voice. Marcus Garvey appealed to racial pride and challenged the concept of equality for all in America. Meanwhile, America was becoming a nation more and more characterized by large cities, and millions of the huddled masses seemed to have strange customs.

America as an urban nation, immigrants pouring in, modern conveniences and new forms of entertainment, political scandals, women's liberation, and aggressive African Americans asserting racial pride—what was happening to the country? What would happen to the time-honored values of rural America? Would respect for God, country, and the family break down? Many people who cherished the old America feared for the worst. They hoped to preserve the old social order, and the methods they used included national prohibition, a hunt for suspected radicals, renewed Ku Klux Klan, resurgent Protestant fundamentalism, and immigration restriction.

What a decade! The economic and social transitions seemed to be opening up new opportunities, while the tensions inherent in such changing times brought out the worst in many people. It was a period rich in social and cultural history, and contemporary writers picked up on the prevailing themes. Perhaps there is always a conflict between those who want to exercise new freedoms and opportunities and those who are opposed. The Great Depression and World War II would divert attention from domestic cultural clashes in the 1930s and 1940s, but the divisions in society over changing values and traditions would recur in post-World War II America.

LEARNING OBJECTIVES

Goal—The purpose of this lesson is to increase our understanding of the economic, social, cultural, and political transitions and tensions characteristic of the 1920s.

Objectives—Upon completion of this lesson, you should be able to:
1. Describe and explain why and how the decade of the 1920s was marked by clashes over social and cultural values.
2. Analyze the changing nature of the American economy and the extent of prosperity during the 1920s.
3. Describe and explain the economic and social significance of the automobile, electricity, and communications advances during the 1920s.
4. Assess the national political leadership and the major political developments of the 1920s.

TEXT FOCUS POINTS

The following questions are designed to help you get the most from your reading. Review them before you do your reading. After completing the assignment, write responses and/or notes to reinforce what you have learned.

Text: Nash et al., *The American People*, Chapter 23, pp. 730-766.

1. How did the Red Scare, the rise of the Ku Klux Klan, and the Sacco and Vanzetti case illustrate the fears and tensions of the early 1920s?
2. What were the signs of prosperity in the 1920s? In what ways did the structure and practice of business change during this period?

3. What was the significance of automobile manufacturing and the automobile itself on the American economy and society in the 1920s?
4. How did the new technology of the era, especially in the areas of electricity and communications, transform American society?
5. How did the Scopes trial and the immigration legislation of the 1920s illustrate reactions to a changing America?
6. What were the effects of the black migration to northern cities? What was the significance of Marcus Garvey?
7. How did the intellectuals of the time, both black and white, express the transitions and tensions of the 1920s?
8. How widespread was the prosperity of the 1920s, particularly among women, farmers, and workers?
9. How would you assess the presidencies of Warren Harding and Calvin Coolidge? What actions characterized American foreign policy during this period?
10. In what ways did progressivism survive in the 1920s? Why did Herbert Hoover win the presidential election of 1928?

VIDEO FOCUS POINTS

The following questions are designed to help you get the most from the video segment of this lesson. Review them before you watch the video. After viewing the video segment, write responses and/or notes to reinforce what you have learned.

Video: "Transitions and Tensions: The 1920s"

1. How does Professor Roderick Nash characterize the 1920s?
2. What were the prevailing political and economic theories of the era? What were the results of putting these theories into practice?
3. What transitions were taking place for women and African Americans? Why did the decade feature prohibition, immigration restriction, Ku Klux Klan activities, and the Scopes trial?
4. What do the transitions and tensions of the 1920s teach us about change in America?
5. What parallels exist between the 1920s and the 1950s? . . . between the 1920s and the 1980s?

ENRICHMENT IDEAS

These activities are not required unless your instructor assigns them. They are offered as suggestions to help you learn more about the material presented in this lesson.

1. Read and analyze the "Recovering the Past" segment on pages 738-739 of *The American People*. Write a report on that segment in which you answer the questions presented in the text.
2. One way to experience the transitions and tensions of the 1920s is to read the literature of the times. Ernest Hemingway's *The Sun Also Rises*, F. Scott Fitzgerald's *The Great Gatsby*, and Claude McKay's *Home to Harlem* represent a sampling of the era. Read one of these novels and then write a critical essay about how well it reflects the times.
3. Read the "Technology Changes the American People" segment about wireless communication on pages 746-747 of your textbook. Write a 750-word essay discussing the questions at the end of the text.

SUGGESTED READINGS

See the "Recommended Reading" listings on page 765 of the text if you wish to explore further the material presented in this lesson.

SUGGESTED WEB SITES

Several places in the textbook will include information marked "The History Place." This is a reference to a related web site. See the "Suggested Web Sites" at the end of the chapter of the textbook if you wish to further explore the material presented in this lesson.

PRACTICE TEST

The following items will help you evaluate your understanding of this lesson. Use the answer key at the end of the lesson to check your answers or to locate material related in each question.

MULTIPLE-CHOICE INSTRUCTIONS

Choose the single best answer. If more than one answer is required, it will be so indicated.

1. The "Red Scare" during 1919-1920 refers to fears that
    A. Indians would reclaim lost lands.
    B. literary works unfairly criticized American society.
    C. Soviets were establishing communism in Cuba.
    D. communist influence was growing in the United States.

2. In economic terms, the period of the 1920s in the United States could be characterized as an era of
    A. agricultural prosperity.
    B. industrial depression.
    C. few technological developments.
    D. industrial revolution.

3. The boom in automobile manufacturing in the 1920s was led by the Ford Motor Company when it
    A. perfected the moving assembly line and mass-production technology.
    B. charged significantly higher prices for their cars in the 1920s than before World War I.
    C. included workers in a management council before making decisions.
    D. demanded that their cars be purchased on a cash-only basis.

4. During the 1920s, sports figures and celebrities like Charles Lindbergh achieved hero status largely because they
    A. appeared in television commercials.
    B. received widespread publicity through new technologies.
    C. provided diversion from wartime problems.
    D. created an escape outlet from the Great Depression.

5. Intolerance during the 1920s in the United States was reflected in the
   A. suppression of the Ku Klux Klan.
   B. passage of restrictive immigration laws.
   C. popularity of jazz.
   D. increased success of labor unions.

6. As a result of black migration to northern cities from 1915 to 1920,
   A. integration of public schools took place peacefully.
   B. southern states escaped racism.
   C. racial tension sometimes erupted as violent riots.
   D. blacks failed to improve their living standard.

7. The Harlem Renaissance is a term that refers to
   A. white American writers who fled to Europe during the 1920s.
   B. black American intellectuals and artists who stressed black pride.
   C. Italian American performers who starred in the opera.
   D. Dutch intellectual movements that greatly influenced American thought.

8. In general, during the 1920s, women in the United States
   A. attempted to have larger families.
   B. involved themselves totally in the "flapper" craze.
   C. spent much less time doing housework.
   D. more often worked outside the home.

9. During the 1920s, the U.S. government
   A. permitted the wealthy to influence policy.
   B. followed the advice of social planners.
   C. generally promoted progressive reform programs.
   D. pursued aggressive regulation of business activities.

10. During the 1920s, progressivism in the United States
    A. enjoyed increasing support.
    B. disappeared altogether.
    C. persisted despite an unfavorable environment.
    D. failed to achieve any important gains.

11. In the video program, Professor Roderick Nash characterized the 1920s as a decade in which
    A. almost everyone drank bootleg gin.
    B. minorities achieved equal opportunities.
    C. society was nervous about changes taking place.
    D. emphasis on domestic affairs made life boring.

12. The prevailing economic thought in the 1920s held that government should
    A. establish price supports for farmers.
    B. tax the rich more aggressively.
    C. create jobs for the unemployed.
    D. free business from regulations.

13. In the video program, Professor Willard Gatewood stated that the Ku Klux Klan gained support in the 1920s because of
    A. financial backing from leading industrialists.
    B. reaction to immigration and urbanization.
    C. lack of moral virtues in the American people.
    D. indifferent attitudes toward law enforcement.

14. During the 1920s, the vast majority of the American people
    A. violated prohibition laws.
    B. adhered to traditional values while accepting moderate change.
    C. believed in fundamentalist teachings.
    D. supported the activities of the Ku Klux Klan.

15. Similarities between the 1920s and the 1950s include all of the following EXCEPT
    A. fears of communist infiltration.
    B. emphasis on material wealth.
    C. weak presidential performance.
    D. tension following world war.

ESSAY/PROBLEM QUESTION

16. Describe and explain how and why the economic, political, social, and cultural developments of the 1920s reflected an era of transition and tension.

ANSWER KEY

Answers	Learning Objectives	Focus Points	References
1. D	1	T1	Nash, p. 732
2. D	2	T2	Nash, p. 736
3. A	3	T3	Nash, pp. 740-742
4. B	3	T4	Nash, pp. 743-745
5. B	1	T5, V3	Nash, pp. 749-751 and Video
6. C	1	T6	Nash, p. 751
7. B	1	T7	Nash, pp. 752-753
8. D	2	T8	Nash, pp. 754-755
9. A	4	T9	Nash, p. 758
10. C	4	T10	Nash, pp. 761-762
11. C	1	V1	Video
12. D	2	V2	Video
13. B	1	V3	Video
14. B	1	V4	Video
15. C	4	V5	Video
16.	All	All	Text and Video

Lesson 13

Hard Times: The Great Depression

LESSON ASSIGNMENTS

Review the following assignments in order to schedule your time appropriately. Pay careful attention; the titles and numbers of the textbook chapter, the telecourse guide lesson, and the video program may be different from one another.

Text: Nash et al., *The American People, Volume Two: From 1865*,
          Chapter 24, "The Great Depression and the New Deal," pp. 768-774.

Reader: *Perspectives on America, Volume 2*,
          "The Days of Boom and Bust," by John Kenneth Galbraith.

Video: "Hard Times: The Great Depression,"
          from the series *America in Perspective*.

OVERVIEW

Like World War I and World War II, the Great Depression of the 1930s had profound effects on the American people. The "hard times" of that era brought forward questions about the nation's economic and political system. On a personal level, the depression was often psychological as well as economic, and the "invisible scars" of the era left deep impressions. The nation and its people were different because of the Great Depression, and those differences are apparent to Americans living sixty years later.

The Great Depression was much more than the stock market crash of late 1929, which is the event we associate with the beginning of the era. The crash was also a symptom of serious problems in the economy. Weak corporate and banking structures, a poor distribution of income, international economic troubles, and poor economic and political leadership all contributed to a downward economic spiral. By the winter of 1932-1933 there was no doubt that the country was in the throes of the most severe economic crisis in its history.

As the depression deepened, people had to cope with it as best they could. For some minority groups, economic conditions were not drastically different. As one contemporary African American observed, "The Negro was born in depression. . . . It only became official when it hit the white man." Many others had not experienced such hardships before, and their reactions varied. Years later, some recalled the camaraderie and sense of helpfulness that developed. Others coped by leaving town, especially men faced with the humiliation of their inability to provide income for their families.

In hindsight, there was relatively little violence associated with the Great Depression. At first, many blamed themselves for their plight. However, as the depression deepened, some began to question the financial and political leadership which had brought them to these harsh conditions. In rural America, ominous signs appeared, as farmers challenged the legal authorities. Most dramatically of all, the Bonus Army of World War I veterans seeking pensions was violently forced out of the nation's capital in the summer of 1932.

President Herbert Hoover drew criticism before the Bonus Army incident, but that event seemed to seal his fate. To his credit, Hoover did use governmental power to attempt to check the depression in a manner unprecedented at that time. However, the Great Depression itself was unparalleled in its severity, and Hoover's actions appeared to be too little, too late. He could never quite break from his belief in rugged individualism and the limits of governmental action. By 1932, Hoover had become the object of ridicule and biting sarcasm.

Rather than turn to violent revolutionary action, people in the United States can use the political system to bring about peaceful change in political leaders and philosophies. Given the conditions prevailing in the presidential election year of 1932, the majority of voters were certain to turn to the Democratic party nominee. The old order of business and political leaders had failed to deal effectively with the economic crisis. The way was cleared for Franklin D. Roosevelt to offer a New Deal to the American people.

LEARNING OBJECTIVES

Goal—The purpose of this lesson is to increase our understanding of the causes and the initial consequences of the Great Depression.

Objectives—Upon completion of this lesson, you should be able to:
1. Describe and explain the causes of the Great Crash and the Great Depression.

2. Examine the initial effects of the depression on the American people and how they coped with the hard times.
3. Analyze President Herbert Hoover's response to the economic crisis facing the nation.
4. Analyze the long-term consequences of the Great Depression.

TEXT FOCUS POINTS

The following questions are designed to help you get the most from your reading. Review them before you do your reading. After completing the assignment, write responses and/or notes to reinforce what you have learned.

Text: Nash et al., *The American People*, Chapter 24, pp. 768-774.

1. After the stock market crash in 1929, why did the nation sink deeper and deeper into depression?
2. How did President Herbert Hoover approach the national economic problems during the early stages of the depression? How did the Federal Farm Board illustrate Hoover's approach?
3. What was the general reaction of the American people to the deepening depression? Who did people blame? How did they cope?
4. What actions did President Hoover take as the depression deepened? What limited his actions?
5. What was the significance of the Bonus Army and the way it was treated?

READER FOCUS QUESTIONS

Reader: *Perspectives on America, Volume 2*, "The Days of Boom and Bust," by Galbraith.

1. Why was income poorly distributed during the 1920s? What effect did that have on the economy?
2. What was the economic effect of the United States' status as a creditor nation after World War I?
3. What were the weaknesses in the corporate structure in the 1920s?

---

4. What explains the stock market boom of the 1920s? What were the inherent dangers in the market?

5. How much blame for the Great Crash and subsequent depression does Professor Galbraith assign to the presidents of the 1920s? What conclusions does he make about the leadership of that era?

VIDEO FOCUS POINTS

The following questions are designed to help you get the most from the video segment of this lesson. Review them before you watch the video. After viewing the video segment, write responses and/or notes to reinforce what you have learned.

Video: "Hard Times: The Great Depression"

1. Why did business and government leaders do so little to prevent the economic collapse associated with the Great Crash and the Great Depression?

2. After the Great Crash, why did the economy continue to worsen?

3. What were the initial reactions of the American people to the depression? How did they cope? What was Hoover's response to the plight of the people? What limited his response?

4. Why didn't the American people take more radical actions during the depression?

5. What were the long-term consequences of the depression on the American people and on the economy?

ENRICHMENT IDEAS

These activities are not required unless your instructor assigns them. They are offered as suggestions to help you learn more abut the material presented in this lesson.

1. Interview some people, preferably family members, about their experiences during the Great Depression. Try to determine how the depression changed their lives and the lives of their descendants. After the interviews, write a 750-word essay in which you describe your own conclusions regarding the effects of the

Great Depression and how people coped. Base your conclusions on the interviews and the material presented in this lesson.

2. Read the book *Hard Times* by Studs Terkel and then write a review of it describing how various people coped with the Great Depression.

SUGGESTED READINGS

See the "Recommended Reading" listings on pages 801-802 of the textbook if you wish to explore further the material presented in this lesson.

SUGGESTED WEB SITES

Several places in the textbook will include information marked "The History Place." This is a reference to a related web site. See the "Suggested Web Sites" at the end of the chapter of the textbook if you wish to further explore the material presented in this lesson.

PRACTICE TEST

The following items will help you evaluate your understanding of this lesson. Use the answer key at the end of the lesson to check your answers or to locate material related in each question.

MULTIPLE-CHOICE INSTRUCTIONS

Choose the single best answer. If more than one answer is required, it will be so indicated.

1. All of the following factors explain why the United States fell deeper and deeper into economic depression in the early 1930s EXCEPT
   A. poorly distributed income.
   B. European goods flooding American markets.
   C. weakened banking and financial institutions.
   D. pessimism and lack of confidence among the people.

2. The Federal Farm Board illustrated President Herbert Hoover's approach to national problems in that it
   A. granted farmers money to cut production.
   B. relied on loans and cooperation.
   C. prevented farm foreclosures.
   D. caused a sharp increase in farm prices.

3. In general, people coped with the hardships of the depression in all of the following ways EXCEPT
   A. helping neighbors as best they could.
   B. seeking relief and food from city and private charity funds.
   C. moving in with relatives.
   D. giving widespread support to revolutionary movements.

4. The attitude of President Hoover toward direct relief for the needy was to
   A. stress private and local responsibility.
   B. generally support federal aid.
   C. expand greatly the aid to veterans.
   D. make many small personal loans.

5. The primary significance of the Bonus Army's march on Washington in 1932 was that the marchers were
   A. successful in lobbying Congress for higher pensions.
   B. infiltrated with large numbers of communists.
   C. supported by General Douglas MacArthur.
   D. forcefully driven out of town after being denied their requests.

6. As a result of poor income distribution in the 1920s, the
   A. labor unions forced workers to strike.
   B. establishment of a welfare system resulted.
   C. economy was heavily dependent on spending by the rich.
   D. government set up work relief programs.

7. One result of the United States being a creditor nation in the 1920s was the
   A. desirability of imports exceeding exports.
   B. collapse of the German Republic.
   C. demand for higher tariff rates.
   D. prohibition of foreign loans.

8. Widespread use of holding companies during the 1920s
    A. promoted corporate stability.
    B. violated the regulations of the stock market.
    C. benefited workers more than speculators.
    D. created a risky foundation for investments.

9. The stock market soared upward in the 1920s in part because
    A. credit was readily available.
    B. sales of securities were closely monitored.
    C. interest rates were averaging three percent.
    D. Democrats regained the presidency.

10. In the article, "The Days of Boom and Bust," John Kenneth Galbraith
    maintained that the Great Crash should teach us that
    A. investment in stocks is foolish.
    B. overregulation of the economy leads to trouble.
    C. high tariff rates are essential.
    D. government works better when leaders respond to criticism.

11. Little occurred to prevent the economic collapse of the Great Depression
    because business and government leaders were
    A. basically incompetent.
    B. too involved to understand the problems.
    C. unable to influence European markets.
    D. overly committed to business regulation.

12. After the Great Crash, the economy continued to worsen because
    A. most Americans had lost fortunes in the market.
    B. deficit financing was practiced by the federal government.
    C. farm prices were too high.
    D. confidence of the people was badly shaken.

13. In the video program, Studs Terkel observed that the American people
    responded relatively moderately to the Great Depression in part because the
    A. initiatives suggested by government solved most problems.
    B. American Dream persisted even during hard times.
    C. alternatives available were unknown.
    D. business establishment seemed to get what it deserved.

14. All of the following were long-term consequences of the Great Depression on the American people EXCEPT that they
    A. continued to be apprehensive about the economy.
    B. established frugal personal habits.
    C. supported laissez-faire economic policies.
    D. approached investments with great caution.

ESSAY/PROBLEM QUESTION

15. Describe and explain at least five major causes of the Great Crash and the Great Depression. How did people cope with the economic crisis? How did President Hoover deal with the crisis? What limited Hoover's actions?

ANSWER KEY

Answers	Learning Objectives	Focus Points	References
1. B	1	T1	Nash, pp. 770
2. B	3	T2	Nash, pp. 770-772
3. D	2	T3, V3	Nash, p. 771 and Video
4. A	3	T4	Nash, pp. 772-773
5. D	3	T5	Nash, pp. 773-774
6. C	1	R1	Reader
7. A	1	R2	Reader
8. D	1	R3	Reader
9. A	1	R4	Reader
10. D	1	R5	Reader
11. B	1	V1	Video
12. D	1	V2	Video
13. B	2	V4	Video
14. C	4	V5	Video
15.	All	All	Text, Reader, and Video

Lesson 14

The New Deal

LESSON ASSIGNMENTS

Review the following assignments in order to schedule your time appropriately. Pay careful attention; the titles and numbers of the textbook chapter, the telecourse guide lesson, and the video program may be different from one another.

Text: Nash et al., *The American People, Volume Two: From 1865,* Chapter 24, "The Great Depression and the New Deal," pp. 774-802.

Video: "The New Deal," from the series *America in Perspective.*

OVERVIEW

When Franklin D. Roosevelt (FDR) became President of the United States on March 4, 1933, the nation was in the midst of its most severe economic depression. Nearly one wage-earner in four was out of work, and states, cities, and private relief agencies were unable to keep pace with the needs for help. In rural America, farmers were burning corn for fuel because of low market prices. Nearly one-fourth of all farmers were losing their farms because they were unable to meet mortgage payments. While other nations facing similar economic depression turned to totalitarianism (e.g., Germany), the people of the United States hoped that their newly elected president would provide effective political leadership. His response would be crucial to the future of the nation.

At first glance, Franklin D. Roosevelt hardly seems to have been a political leader who would inspire hope among the underclass. He was the product of an upper-class background, and he had offered little in the way of specifics during the 1932 presidential campaign. Unlike Herbert Hoover, however, FDR disavowed any strict adherence to a political philosophy which might place limits on his freedom of action. He offered "a new deal for the American people."

Roosevelt's political philosophy was much less important to people in 1933

---

than what he would actually do about the Great Depression. It was in this vital area that FDR's experimental approach and confident style would strike a responsive chord. In his first inaugural address he assured the people "that the only thing we have to fear is fear itself." The next day he issued two orders—one called Congress into special session and the other proclaimed a bank holiday. One week later he addressed the nation in the first of his "fireside chats." FDR reassured the people that their money would be safe in the newly reopened banks. Raymond Moley, a presidential adviser, concluded that "capitalism was saved in eight days."

It was not quite that simple, for much was yet to be done. Most historians divide the New Deal into phases, with the emphasis on "relief and recovery" during the first New Deal and on more permanent "reform" during the second New Deal. While these descriptions are helpful, it is perhaps even more important to grasp the totality of the New Deal programs. They affected every sector of the American economy and population. Farmers, workers, minorities, the unemployed, the elderly—all now had a different relationship with the federal government. Moreover, the resulting formation of a New Deal Political Coalition translated into an unprecedented four presidential election victories for FDR.

Although historians have argued about how liberal or conservative Franklin D. Roosevelt and the New Deal were, there is no doubt that the political landscape was transformed. The New Dealers added the concept of guarantor, which had been espoused by the earlier progressives, to the role of the federal government. FDR declared as much in his annual message to Congress in 1938:

> Government has a final responsibility for the well-being of its citizenship. If private cooperative endeavor fails to provide work for willing hands and relief for the unfortunate, those suffering hardship from no fault of their own have a right to call upon the government for aid; and a government worthy of its name must make a fitting response.

Franklin D. Roosevelt and his New Deal programs did not end the economic depression, but they did leave a significant political legacy. The federal government's role in American life was permanently altered. For better or for worse, the American people now expected the government, and particularly the president, to respond to pressing economic and social needs. The specific legislation regarding business, labor, farmers, and everyone else may have been altered in subsequent years, but the basic foundation has not been destroyed. The proposition that the government is, to a large degree, responsible for the social and economic well-being of its people became a new political tradition.

LEARNING OBJECTIVES

Goal—The purpose of this lesson is to increase our understanding of 1) how President Franklin D. Roosevelt and the New Deal responded to the crisis of the Great Depression, and 2) the consequences of those responses.

Objectives—Upon completion of this lesson, you should be able to:
1. Describe and explain the responses of Franklin D. Roosevelt and the New Deal to specific issues of the 1930s, particularly unemployment, income distribution, labor, farmers, minorities, banking, and business regulation.
2. Evaluate the long-term significance of FDR and the New Deal in respect to American politics and to the relationship of the federal government with the people.
3. Discuss the significant social and cultural developments of the 1930s.

TEXT FOCUS POINTS

The following questions are designed to help you get the most from your reading. Review them before you do your reading. After completing the assignment, write responses and/or notes to reinforce what you have learned.

Text: Nash et al., *The American People,* Chapter 24, pp. 774-802.

1. Describe FDR's political philosophy and his personal leadership qualities. What effect did Eleanor Roosevelt have on presidential policy?
2. What were the short- and long-term effects of actions taken during the first New Deal (1933-34) regarding banking, emergency relief, agriculture, business, labor, and conservation?
3. Who were FDR's critics during his first term and what were the effects of their criticism?
4. What was the major emphasis of the second New Deal? What actions were taken regarding work relief, social security, farmers, and corporations? Describe the causes and effects of the "dust bowl."

5. What is the significance of the Wagner (National Labor Relations) Act? What significant developments took place in the union movement during the mid-1930s?

6. To what extent was there a "new deal" for American minorities during the 1930s?

7. Why did FDR win the presidential election of 1936? What resulted from his efforts to pack the Supreme Court? How did Roosevelt respond when the American economy began to slump again in 1937?

8. What were the results of the housing legislation and the Fair Labor Standards Act (1938) of the third New Deal?

9. How did technological advances affect life in the 1930s? What did the major literary works of the time say about the era? What were the effects of radio and the movies during the 1930s?

VIDEO FOCUS POINTS

The following questions are designed to help you get the most from the video segment of this lesson. Review them before you watch the video. After viewing the video segment, write responses and/or notes to reinforce what you have learned.

Video: "The New Deal"

1. Why did Franklin D. Roosevelt win the presidential election of 1932?

2. What were the effects of the actions taken by FDR and the New Deal in regard to banking, relief programs, and farming? From whom did FDR draw criticism? What were the effects of those criticisms?

3. What were the immediate and long-term effects of the actions taken by FDR and the New Deal regarding workers? What actions were taken regarding African Americans? What limited FDR's actions in that regard?

4. What political tradition shaped FDR's view of the presidency? How did he change the presidency?

5. What were the long-term effects of the New Deal? How was it linked to the progressive era? What did it illustrate about the American political system?

ENRICHMENT IDEAS

These activities are not required unless your instructor assigns them. They are offered as suggestions to help you learn more about the material presented in this lesson. ✓

1. In a well-reasoned, 750-word essay, identify the three greatest and the three worst presidents of the United States since 1877. Explain fully, giving a complete rationale for your selections and drawing conclusions regarding what determines a president's success or failure.
2. FDR was quoted as saying, "We ought to have two real parties—one liberal and one conservative." Describe and explain the advantages and/or disadvantages of such a party realignment and state your own conclusions about the proposal.
3. Read and analyze the "Recovering the Past" segment on pages 796-797 of *The American People*. Write a report on that segment in which you answer the questions presented in the text.
4. Read the article entitled "Shut the Goddam Plant," in *Perspectives on America, Volume 2*. Then write a 750-word essay in which you analyze the reasons for the strike, the tactics used by the union, and the results of the strike.

SUGGESTED READINGS

See the "Recommended Reading" listings on pages 801-802 of the text if you wish to explore further the material presented in this lesson.

SUGGESTED WEB SITES

Several places in the textbook will include information marked "The History Place." This is a reference to a related web site. See the "Suggested Web Sites" at the end of the chapter of the textbook if you wish to further explore the material presented in this lesson.

PRACTICE TEST

The following items will help you evaluate your understanding of this lesson. Use the answer key at the end of the lesson to check your answers or to locate material related in each question.

MULTIPLE-CHOICE INSTRUCTIONS

Choose the single best answer. If more than one answer is required, it will be so indicated.

1. In establishing New Deal policies, Franklin Roosevelt
   A. adhered to rigid philosophic principles.
   B. revealed little understanding of the average American.
   C. showed contempt for conservative traditions.
   D. exhibited a flexible approach to solving problems.

2. The National Industrial Recovery Act (NIRA) did all of the following EXCEPT
   A. give the NRA power to establish fair pricing codes.
   B. recognize labor's right to organize and bargain collectively.
   C. emphasize cooperation rather than competition.
   D. win the approval of the Supreme Court.

3. Opposition to the New Deal came mostly from
   A. farmers.
   B. conservative labor leaders.
   C. extreme left-wingers and extreme right-wingers.
   D. poorer elements of the South.

4. Relative to the first New Deal, the second New Deal
   A. promoted fewer programs for social reform.
   B. focused on economic rather than social reform.
   C. included more cooperation with American business.
   D. reflected the demand for more social justice.

5. All of the following were characteristic of the union movement during the 1930s EXCEPT
   A. organizational growth, especially by the CIO.
   B. "sit-down strikes" as a protest activity.
   C. lower status for organized labor.
   D. recognition by GM, Ford, and Chrysler after strong resistance.

6. During the New Deal, African Americans
   A. benefited equally with whites from relief programs.
   B. viewed Eleanor Roosevelt as an opponent of racial justice.
   C. gained FDR's backing for strong civil rights laws.
   D. received more government recognition than previously.

7. Franklin Roosevelt created the strongest opposition to his administration when he
   A. interfered in state elections.
   B. advocated social security legislation.
   C. defended the National Recovery Administration.
   D. attempted to change the make-up of the Supreme Court.

8. The housing legislation promoted by the New Deal
   A. eliminated the country's housing shortage.
   B. favored the purchase of suburban homes.
   C. addressed only slums in the central city.
   D. affected primarily the unemployed.

9. During the Great Depression, in general, movies
   A. explored the more serious aspects of American culture.
   B. provided an escape from the reality of economic conditions.
   C. provided entertainment only for the upper classes.
   D. created little impact on American lifestyles.

10. FDR won the presidential election of 1932 because the electorate
    A. wanted to avoid a revolution.
    B. rejected the policies and approach of Herbert Hoover.
    C. accepted his carefully thought-out plan for recovery.
    D. disapproved of the scandals associated with the incumbent.

11. In the video program, Professor Arthur M. Schlesinger pointed out that FDR was shaped by a political tradition which stressed
    A. strong and affirmative presidential actions.
    B. parliamentary-style government.
    C. laissez-faire policies.
    D. appeasing the upper classes.

12. The New Deal was linked to the progressive era in the respect that
    A. income tax rates on the rich were lowered.
    B. many leaders of the 1930s grew up politically in the earlier period.
    C. neither era could pull minority votes away from the Republican party.
    D. both occurred during depression times.

ESSAY/PROBLEM QUESTIONS

13. Describe and explain the actions taken by Franklin D. Roosevelt and the New Deal in reference to farmers, labor, business, minorities, and income distribution. What was the long-term significance of those actions?

14. Describe and explain how and why Franklin D. Roosevelt and the New Deal changed the course of American politics. In your answer be sure to consider the presidency, political parties, and the role of the federal government in American life.

ANSWER KEY

Answers	Learning Objectives	Focus Points	References
1.	D	1	T1	Nash, pp. 776-777
2.	D	1	T2	Nash, p. 779
3.	C	1	T3, V2	Nash, pp. 780-781 and Video
4.	D	2	T4	Nash, pp. 781-783
5.	C	2	T5	Nash, pp. 785-787
6.	D	1	T6, V3	Nash, pp. 787-788 and Video
7.	D	2	T7	Nash, pp. 791-792
8.	B	1	T8	Nash, p. 792
9.	B	3	T9	Nash, pp. 799-800
10.	B	1	V1	Video
11.	A	2	V4	Video
12.	B	2	V5	Video
13.		All	All	Text and Video
14.		All	All	Text and Video

Lesson 15

The Road to War

LESSON ASSIGNMENTS

Review the following assignments in order to schedule your time appropriately. Pay careful attention; the titles and numbers of the textbook chapter, the telecourse guide lesson, and the video program may be different from one another.

Text: Nash et al., *The American People, Volume Two: From 1865*, Chapter 25, "World War II," pp. 804-825.

Reader: *Perspectives on America, Volume 2*, "Man of the Century," by Arthur Schlesinger, Jr.

Video: "The Road to War," from the series *America in Perspective*.

OVERVIEW

The refusal of the United States to join the League of Nations at the end of World War I indicated that the interests of the nation would be directed toward domestic life. Certainly the transitions and tensions of the 1920s and the traumas of the Great Depression of the 1930s occupied the lives of most Americans. However, it would be a misconception to think that the United States totally dropped out of world affairs in 1920 and remained isolated until the nation entered World War II in 1941. Rather, the United States continued to search for world markets and economic influence, especially since World War I had made the United States the world's leading creditor nation. Furthermore, although it was operating outside the League of Nations, the United States still confronted the issues of international communism, disarmament, its strained relations with Latin American countries, and, eventually, renewed aggression in Europe, Africa, and Asia.

By the mid-1930s, actions taken by Germany, Italy, and Japan threatened world peace. In response, Congress proceeded to pass three neutrality acts which represented a retreat from the freedom of the seas and neutral rights which the United States had insisted upon prior to World War I. In fact, the chief fault with the neutrality acts may have been that they were intended to keep the United States out of a war it had already fought—that is, the United States was attempting to apply the lessons of pre-World War I diplomacy to the 1930s. However, the situation in the 1930s was not the same—the enemies were more dangerous, and the lessons did not apply directly.

By September 1939, the aggressive actions of Germany and Italy had led to the outbreak of war once again in Europe. Following tradition and policy, President Franklin D. Roosevelt (FDR) proclaimed neutrality for the United States. Almost immediately, however, the United States began to compromise its strict neutrality by aiding the British and French in their struggle against the Axis powers. By March 1941, the United States had approved the Lend-Lease Act, called "an economic declaration of war" by some historians. By late summer, U.S. warships were escorting lend-lease shipments overseas. Clashes with German submarines appeared inevitable.

Of course, the ultimate blow which finally brought the United States officially into the shooting war came halfway around the world from the raging European conflict. Japanese aggression in the Far East had in effect closed the Open Door in China. In response, the United States imposed economic sanctions against the Japanese. By 1941, the sanctions had progressed from the restrictions on the sale of airplanes, aviation gasoline, scrap metals, and machine tools to the freezing of Japanese assets in the United States and an embargo on oil. Negotiations regarding U.S.-Japanese relations were still going on when suddenly, on the morning of December 7, 1941, the Japanese attacked the U.S. Naval Base at Pearl Harbor on the Hawaiian Islands. It was a date, FDR told Congress, "which will live in infamy."

Thus, Pearl Harbor was the last link in a chain of events which had led the United States into World War II. It was apparent to most leaders that this was not going to be a replay of World War I. The enemies were more threatening and more powerful. This war would be longer and more costly in terms of money and lives, requiring greater concentration of resources and greater regimentation of lives at home. Consequently, the role of the federal government, already expanded by the depression of the 1930s, took on even greater dimensions during the war. At the same time, war production demands ended the unemployment so characteristic of the 1930s and opened up new economic opportunities for millions of Americans. Still other Americans—some 16 million of them—served in the armed forces, including many women who joined newly organized women's branches of the military.

While the Japanese attack on Pearl Harbor brought the United States into the war and had some long-term effects on national security planning, its immediate effects were to unify the American people—and to help justify the internment of some 112,000 Japanese Americans. The American Civil Liberties Union, one of the few organizations to protest the move, called this action "the greatest single assault on the Constitution in the nation's history." At the very least, the branding of Japanese Americans, citizens and aliens alike, as "an enemy race" represented "the culmination of a long history of anti-Asian bigotry as well as a severe case of war hysteria." (*We Americans: A Topical History of the United States,* Glenview, Ill.: Scott Foresman, 1976, p. 608)

With the mobilization of the American mind and the American economy, the United States was rapidly becoming the "arsenal of democracy." Indeed, American resources would be a key to the ultimate defeat of the Axis powers. Most Americans now seemed ready to get on with the war, a war that would fundamentally change the American people and the American nation.

LEARNING OBJECTIVES

Goal—The purpose of this lesson is to increase our understanding of the diplomatic road to World War II, the reaction to the Japanese attack on Pearl Harbor, and the effects of wartime mobilization on the American people.

Objectives—Upon completing this lesson, you should be able to:
1. Describe and explain the main features of American foreign policy from the end of World War I to the attack on Pearl Harbor.
2. Analyze the short-term and long-term effects of the Pearl Harbor attack on the American people and American policy.
3. Examine the process of wartime mobilization and its effects on the American economy.
4. Analyze the effects of World War II on racial and ethnic minorities and women in the United States.
5. Describe and explain the social effects of the war on society in general.

TEXT FOCUS POINTS

The following questions are designed to help you get the most from your reading. Review them before you do your reading. After completing the assignment, write responses and/or notes to reinforce what you have learned.

Text: Nash et al., *The American People*, Chapter 25, pp. 804-825.

1. How did FDR carry out the Good Neighbor Policy?
2. What explains American domestic and foreign policy reactions to world developments prior to the outbreak of war in Europe in 1939? What were the provisions of the neutrality legislation passed in the mid-1930s?
3. How and why did the United States compromise its neutrality before entering World War II?
4. What was Roosevelt's role in the Japanese attack on Pearl Harbor? What were the effects of the Japanese attack on Pearl Harbor?
5. How successful was Roosevelt in mobilizing America for war? How did World War II affect the American economy?
6. What factors explain the internment of Japanese Americans?
7. How did World War II affect African Americans and Hispanics?
8. How was domestic life in general affected by the war?
9. What effects did the war have on women?
10. What were the effects of the war on American GIs?

READER FOCUS POINTS

Reader: *Perspectives on America, Volume 2*, "Man of the Century," by Schlesinger.

1. What factors shaped FDR's approach to world affairs?
2. In FDR's thinking, how would World War II transform the world? Why does the author think that "the world we live in today is Franklin Roosevelt's world?"

VIDEO FOCUS POINTS

The following questions are designed to help you get the most from the video segment of this lesson. Review them before you watch the video. After viewing the video segment, write responses and/or notes to reinforce what you have learned.

Video: "The Road to War"

1. Why did the American people want to withdraw from world affairs in the 1920s and 1930s? Why was it difficult to do so?
2. How did the leaders of the United States try to apply the lessons of World War I to the developments leading up to the outbreak of World War II? Why did these efforts fail to keep the United States out of the second war?
3. Why was the United States caught by surprise at Pearl Harbor? What were the immediate and long-term effects of the Pearl Harbor attack?
4. What were the immediate and long-term effects of war mobilization on American society? What role was the United States to play in the Allied strategy to win the war?
5. Why were Japanese Americans forced into internment camps? Why were such violations of civil liberties permitted?

ENRICHMENT IDEAS

This activity is not required unless your instructor assigns it. It is offered as a suggestion to help you learn more about the material presented in this lesson.

1. Read and analyze the "Recovering the Past" segment on pages 832-833 of *The American People*. Using the suggested questions in the textbook, interview a family member who clearly remembers World War II. Then write a 750-word report in which you summarize what you have learned about how World War II affected your family.
2. Read the "Technology Changes the American People" segment about the invention of plastics on pages 812-813 of your textbook. Write a 750-word essay discussing the questions at the end of the text.

SUGGESTED READINGS

See the "Recommended Reading" listings on pages 836-837 of the text if you wish to explore further the material presented in this lesson.

SUGGESTED WEB SITES

Several places in the textbook will include information marked "The History Place." This is a reference to a related web site. See the "Suggested Web Sites" at the end of the chapter of the textbook if you wish to further explore the material presented in this lesson.

PRACTICE TEST

The following items will help you evaluate your understanding of this lesson. Use the answer key at the end of the lesson to check your answers or to locate material related in each question.

MULTIPLE-CHOICE INSTRUCTIONS

Choose the single best answer. If more than one answer is required, it will be so indicated.

1. In relations with Latin America during the Franklin Roosevelt administration, the United States
   A. implemented the Roosevelt Corollary to the Monroe Doctrine.
   B. reversed the earlier policy of intervention.
   C. intervened in Cuba to protect American investments.
   D. ceased relations with Mexico over nationalization of American oil companies.

2. U.S. neutrality legislation in the mid-1930s contained all of the following provisions EXCEPT
   A. enacting an arms embargo.
   B. selling nonmilitary items to belligerents on a cash basis.
   C. forgiving World War I war debts.
   D. prohibiting travel for citizens on belligerent ships.

3. After his reelection in 1940, Franklin Roosevelt's response to the developments in Europe was to
   A. maintain strict neutrality.
   B. help Germany without involving the United States in the war.
   C. aid the British war effort by supporting the Lend-Lease Act.
   D. carefully plan a strategy to deal with war in Europe.

4. The Japanese attack on Pearl Harbor
   A. united the country behind the war effort.
   B. revealed a conspiracy within the Roosevelt administration.
   C. ruined FDR's reelection chances.
   D. prompted the United States to pass the Lend-Lease Act.

5. One effect of World War II on the American economy was that it
   A. retarded growth of labor unions.
   B. created the basis for the development of a military-industrial complex.
   C. lowered tax rates.
   D. loosened government control over the economy.

6. During World War II, the ethnic group living in the United States that faced the most difficult test of loyalty was the
   A. Germans.
   B. Italians.
   C. Russians.
   D. Japanese.

7. For Mexican Americans, World War II created
   A. few changes in lifestyle.
   B. a time when they faced little discrimination.
   C. increased economic opportunity.
   D. threat of deportation.

8. World War II affected American society by
   A. decreasing the educational level of the American people.
   B. increasing the mobility of the American people.
   C. eliminating prejudice among the American people.
   D. spurring a movement back to small towns and farms.

9. During World War II, the new women war workers in the United States were
   A. excluded from seemingly "unladylike" work in heavy industry.
   B. almost exclusively single.
   C. more likely to be married than single.
   D. paid wages equal to men.

10. Black American soldiers during World War II
    A. served in integrated units.
    B. faced little prejudice from white soldiers.
    C. suffered a higher percentage of casualties than white soldiers.
    D. discovered the paradox of fighting for freedom when they enjoyed little freedom.

11. All of the following factors shaped FDR's approach to world affairs EXCEPT his
    A. desire to appease corporate capitalists in the United States.
    B. broad international experience.
    C. admiration for President Theodore Roosevelt's grasp of geopolitics.
    D. respect for President Woodrow Wilson's vision of a world beyond war.

12. The world of today seems to be the world envisioned by FDR in all of the following ways EXCEPT the
    A. emergence of China as a major factor in world affairs.
    B. refusal of Russia to permit capitalist ventures internally.
    C. democratic movements in Eastern Europe.
    D. continued pursuit of peace and cooperation by the United Nations.

13. Americans found it difficult to withdraw from world affairs in the mid-1930s because
   A. congressional investigations supported intervention.
   B. totalitarian nations awakened political interest.
   C. FDR continued to wield the big stick in Latin America.
   D. military alliances required troop deployments.

14. An immediate effect of World War II on America was the
   A. abolition of racial segregation.
   B. election of a Republican president.
   C. creation of an all-volunteer army.
   D. stimulation of the economy.

15. During wartime, Americans seem to tolerate violations of civil liberties because they
   A. admire a strong president.
   B. support suspension of the Constitution.
   C. fear being labeled unpatriotic.
   D. think the American Civil Liberties Union is too radical.

ESSAY/PROBLEM QUESTIONS

16. Describe and explain the major foreign policy decisions of the United States between 1921 and the Japanese attack on Pearl Harbor. Why were American efforts to avoid another war unsuccessful?

17. How did the mobilization of the United States for participation in World War II affect American society in general and the American economy in particular? In your answer, be sure to consider both short- and long-term effects.

ANSWER KEY

Answers	Learning Objectives	Focus Points	References
1. B	1	T1	Nash, pp. 806-807
2. C	1	T2, V2	Nash, pp. 807-808 and Video
3. C	1	T3	Nash, p. 810
4. A	2	T4, V3	Nash, pp. 810-811 and p. 814; Video
5. B	3	T5	Nash, pp. 814-816
6. D	4	T6	Nash, pp. 816-818
7. C	4	T7	Nash, pp. 819-820
8. B	5	T8	Nash, p. 820
9. C	4	T9	Nash, pp. 821-822
10. D	5	T10	Nash, p.824
11. A	1	R1	Reader
12. B	2	R2	Reader
13. B	1	V1	Video
14. D	3	V4	Video
15. C	4	V5	Video
16.	All	All	Text, Reader, and Video
17.	All	All	Text, Reader, and Video

Lesson 16

The Good War

LESSON ASSIGNMENTS

Review the following assignments in order to schedule your time appropriately. Pay careful attention; the titles and numbers of the textbook chapter, the telecourse guide lesson, and the video program may be different from one another.

Text: Nash et al., *The American People, Volume Two: From 1865*, Chapter 25, "World War II," pp. 825-837.

Video: "The Good War," from the series *America in Perspective.*

OVERVIEW

On December 7, 1991, Americans commemorated the fiftieth anniversary of the Japanese attack on Pearl Harbor. For the generation that experienced World War II, that incident marked the beginning of a series of events that touched their lives very deeply. For those who survived, "the war" became a point of reference. For the United States, it became the key in the transformation of the nation into the military superpower that it has remained ever since.

Of course, in 1941 few people took the time to reflect upon what World War II would mean to the American people and the nation in the long run. They were more concerned with the immediate task at hand, which was to defeat Japan and the other Axis powers as quickly as possible. At first, the main emphasis of the U.S. military effort was directed at Hitler's Germany. This strategy was in accord with the wishes of Great Britain and the Soviet Union, who feared that if the United States diverted its main strength to the Pacific, Hitler might prove unconquerable. When Germany was defeated, they reasoned that the combined Allied forces could be turned on Japan. Thus, enough American military strength was sent to the Pacific to keep Japan busy, but concentration was initially placed in the European theater of operations.

After hard-fought and costly Allied successes in North Africa, Italy, and the Soviet Union, the D-Day invasion on June 6, 1944, finally put Hitler and his military forces in a vise from which they could not escape. The Allied advance on western Germany, occurring simultaneously with Russian movements on the east and the incessant bombing of the German interior, had Hitler reeling by 1945. The public now became aware of the extent of the incredible German atrocities against the Jews, as Allied forces liberated concentration camp survivors, found mass graves, and exposed Nazi methods of mass murder. Finally, Hitler, convinced that most of his staff had turned against him and with Russian troops entering Berlin, married his mistress and committed suicide with her in an underground bunker on April 30, 1945. One week later, what was left of the German government surrendered unconditionally. The next day, May 8, 1945, was officially proclaimed V-E (Victory in Europe) Day—to the frenzied delight of the Allied countries.

In February 1945, the Big Three (Franklin Roosevelt, Winston Churchill, and Joseph Stalin) met at Yalta, a resort town in the Russian Crimea. There they reached agreements on the fate of Germany, the settlement of boundary and political questions in postwar Eastern Europe, the prosecution of the war against Japan, and the establishment of the United Nations. The significance of the Yalta Conference is difficult to overemphasize, for the decisions made there affected the world for decades afterward.

One arrangement made at Yalta was that the Soviet Union would join the war against Japan three months after the war in Europe had ended. At the time of that agreement, American officials believed that Soviet forces could help save American lives in what still appeared to be a difficult and costly struggle to defeat Japan. As it turned out, the American use of the atomic bombs against Japan hastened the end of a tremendously destructive war.

What was not over, however, were the effects of the changes brought about by World War II. On a personal level, "the war" had left an indelible mark on the lives of those who survived it. In addition, the American people could take solace from the fact that the nation had faced the challenge of totalitarian aggression and had emerged triumphant. The bombing of Pearl Harbor had brought about an all-out war effort, in which the nation's material and human resources were mobilized to the fullest extent. The strength that the United States was able to employ had been the turning point in the war. At the end of the war, the United States stood towering above the war-ravaged world. The "superpower" had emerged, and this time there would be no turning back from the responsibilities of world leadership.

LEARNING OBJECTIVES

Goal—The purpose of this lesson is to increase our understanding of the military and diplomatic aspects of World War II and the effects of that war on the American people and the place of the United States in the world.

Objectives—Upon completion of this lesson, you should be able to:
1. Describe and explain the Allied strategy for defeating the Axis powers.
2. Examine the diplomatic decisions and military operations which led to the defeat of Germany and Japan.
3. Analyze the significance of the Yalta agreements and the development and use of the atomic bombs.
4. Evaluate the effects of World War II on American society and on the shape of the postwar world.

TEXT FOCUS POINTS

The following questions are designed to help you get the most from your reading. Review them before you do your reading. After completing the assignment, write responses and/or notes to reinforce what you have learned.

Text: Nash et al., *The American People*, Chapter 25, pp. 825-837.

1. What were the aims of the United States in World War II? What was the initial strategy for fighting the war against both Germany and Japan?
2. What factors made 1942 a difficult year for the United States and its Allies? What limited any actions to help the Jews in Europe?
3. What were General Dwight Eisenhower's strengths as a commander? How much progress had the Allies made toward defeating the Axis powers by 1944?
4. What was the significance of Operation Overlord? What were the effects of the bombing of Germany? What were the strengths and weaknesses of the American army units compared to the Germans?
5. Explain the arrangements which were made at the Yalta Conference.
6. Why were the atomic bombs used against Japan? What were the results of the use of the bombs?

VIDEO FOCUS POINTS

The following questions are designed to help you get the most from the video segment of this lesson. Review them before you watch the video. After viewing the video segment, write responses and/or notes to reinforce what you have learned.

Video: "The Good War"

1. What factors shaped Allied strategy in World War II? Why did the Allies insist on unconditional surrender? What were the consequences of that decision?
2. Why does Professor Stephen Ambrose consider the success of the D-Day invasion "the turning point in the second world war"? How important was General Dwight Eisenhower in that operation?
3. What limited American actions regarding German concentration camps prior to their liberation in 1945? What effects did the Holocaust have on the United States?
4. How did the arrangements made at Yalta reflect the realities of that time? Why were those arrangements controversial later?
5. Why did the United States use atomic bombs in August 1945? What were the effects of the use of atomic weapons?
6. What were the effects of World War II on the American spirit, the economy, civil rights, and the relations of the United States with the rest of the world?

ENRICHMENT IDEAS

These activities are not required unless your instructor assigns them. They are offered as suggestions to help you learn more about the material presented in this lesson.

1. After reading and analyzing the "Recovering the Past" segment on pages 832-833 of *The American People,* interview a veteran of World War II. Then write a 750-word report in which you summarize what you have learned about how the wartime experience affected the life of the person you interviewed.
2. Read the article, "The Biggest Decision: Why We Had to Drop the Atomic Bomb," in *Perspectives on America, Volume 2.* Then write a 750-word essay in which you summarize the article and state and defend your position on whether or not the United States was justified in using the atomic bombs against Japan.

SUGGESTED READINGS

See the "Recommended Reading" listings on pages 836-837 of the text if you wish to explore further the material presented in this lesson.

SUGGESTED WEB SITES

Several places in the textbook will include information marked "The History Place." This is a reference to a related web site. See the "Suggested Web Sites" at the end of the chapter of the textbook if you wish to further explore the material presented in this lesson.

PRACTICE TEST

The following items will help you evaluate your understanding of this lesson. Use the answer key at the end of the lesson to check your answers or to locate material related in each question.

MULTIPLE-CHOICE INSTRUCTIONS

Choose the single best answer. If more than one answer is required, it will be so indicated.

1. Allied strategists in World War II decided to concentrate their forces against the
   A. Japanese before challenging the Germans.
   B. threat of a German invasion of the Soviet Union.
   C. possibility that Germany might invade the United States.
   D. Germans first.

2. All of the following factors made 1942 a difficult year for the Allies EXCEPT
   A. Japan made significant advances in the Pacific theater.
   B. Russian territory was invaded by Germans.
   C. American reporters detailed every American defeat.
   D. German forces in North Africa threatened the Suez Canal.

3. By 1944, Allied progress toward defeating the Axis powers was indicated by all of the following EXCEPT
   A. Germany's withdrawal from Italy.
   B. Allied invasion of Italy.
   C. American success in retaking some territory from Japan.
   D. Italian surrender after overthrowing Mussolini.

4. Allied bombing of Germany
   A. created tremendous damage in cities.
   B. destroyed German morale.
   C. totally disrupted German war production.
   D. occurred with little resistance.

5. At the Yalta Conference, President Franklin Roosevelt
   A. was outsmarted by Joseph Stalin.
   B. refused to make concessions to the Soviets in Asia.
   C. requested Soviet help in ending the war in the Pacific.
   D. demanded that the Soviets leave Eastern Europe.

6. The primary reason for using the atomic bombs against Japan was to
   A. demonstrate that the bombs would work.
   B. illustrate President Truman's leadership.
   C. fulfill an agreement made at Yalta.
   D. force Japan to surrender without an Allied invasion.

7. One of FDR's prime concerns regarding Allied strategy was
   A. liberating the Jews.
   B. relieving Russian forces.
   C. saving American lives.
   D. removing Stalin from power.

8. In the video program, Professor Stephen Ambrose stated that the success of the D-Day invasion was "the turning point" in World War II because
   A. Stalin and Hitler had already negotiated an end to the war.
   B. German atrocities against the Jews were finally revealed.
   C. German military leaders surrendered without a fight.
   D. failure there might have meant losing the war.

9. The United States was limited in its ability to liberate concentration camps in 1945 because
   A. intelligence regarding their existence was inaccurate.
   B. agreements made previously with Hitler prohibited action.
   C. Yalta agreements required Russia to free the camps.
   D. Germany controlled the locations of the camps.

10. Actions by A. Philip Randolph during World War II indicated that minorities could
    A. attend the schools of their choice at war's end.
    B. not expect any improvement in conditions.
    C. make gains through organization and pressure.
    D. vote without restrictions in presidential elections.

ESSAY/PROBLEM QUESTIONS

11. Analyze the importance of American military forces, political and military leaders, and industry in the defeat of the Axis powers in World War II. How did the war change the shape of the world and the place of the United States in international affairs?

12. Describe and explain the arrangements made at the Yalta Conference and assess the short- and long-term consequences of those arrangements.

ANSWER KEY

Answers	Learning Objectives	Focus Points	References
1. D	1	T1	Nash, pp. 825-826
2. C	2	T2	Nash, pp. 826-829
3. A	2	T3	Nash, p. 829
4. A	2	T4	Nash, p. 830
5. C	3	T5, V4	Nash, pp. 831 and 834; Video
6. D	3	T6, V5	Nash, pp. 834-836 and Video
7. C	1	V1	Video
8. D	2	V2	Video
9. D	2	V3	Video
10. C	4	V6	Video
11.	All	All	Text and Video
12.	All	All	Text and Video

Unit Three:
A Resilient People
Since 1945

Resilience refers to the ability to return to an original form after being bent, compressed, or stretched or the power to recover from some adversity. In the years since 1945, the American people have been challenged to live up to their ideals and to adapt to changing economic, social, political, and diplomatic realities. For most of the era, the Cold War dominated world affairs. At times, attempts to contain the perceived communist menace resulted in actions which ran counter to America's historic mission in the world and tested the limits of American power. Yet the ultimate collapse of the Soviet Union confirmed for many the belief that democracy and capitalism would inevitably triumph. At home, the Watergate affair stretched the limits of politics before ending with restored faith in the checks and balances system. Meanwhile, minorities demanded that they too should finally share equally in the American Dream and insisted that their cultures deserved respect. Concerns with education, crime, health, the environment, and a pervasive national debt are sure to continue to challenge the American people. To meet those challenges, we Americans will need to draw upon the strengths of our heritage.

Lesson 17

The Cold War Begins

LESSON ASSIGNMENTS

Review the following assignments in order to schedule your time appropriately. Pay careful attention; the titles and numbers of the textbook chapter, the telecourse guide lesson, and the video program may be different from one another.

Text: Nash et al., *The American People, Volume Two: From 1865,*
Chapter 27, "Chills and Fever During the Cold War," pp. 872-895.

Reader: *Perspectives on America, Volume 2,*
"Leaving for Korea," by James Brady.

Video: "The Cold War Begins,"
from the series *America in Perspective.*

OVERVIEW

In 1945, at the end of World War II, the United States stood at the pinnacle of world power. It had a large battle-tested army, a navy more powerful than all the other fleets in the world combined, an air force greater than any other ever assembled, and of course, sole possession of the atomic bomb—the "ultimate weapon." Besides, the strength of the United States was not just military. In economic terms, the power of the United States was also unmatched. The nation seemed to be perfectly positioned to continue its mission to spread democracy and capitalism throughout the world.

With all of this national power, the people of the United States might have been expected to enjoy an era of confidence and security. Instead, the years after 1945 were often marked by a sense of doubt and insecurity in foreign affairs. At the base of this apprehension in the midst of power was the reaction of the United States to the forces of international communism. Soon after the war ended, one of our key wartime allies became an ominous enemy. The globe quickly became divided between the so-called Free World (the United States and its allies) and the

Communist Bloc (the Soviet Union and its allies), with other countries pressured to choose one of the two sides. There developed a Cold War, in which the tension and hostility between the two sides matched that of a wartime crisis, although the two never challenged each other directly in an all-out shooting confrontation.

The origins of the Cold War can be traced at least as far back as the Communist Revolution in Russia in 1917. What caused the inherent conflict between capitalism and communism to intensify in the immediate post-World War II years, however, has been a matter of some controversy. Some historians believe that the actions of the United States at the end of World War II had almost as much to do with the development of the Cold War as did the behavior of the Soviet Union. Whatever the case, each country's perception of the other led to a series of decisions which seemed at times to threaten the very survival of the planet.

The policy of the United States toward the Soviet Union was given clear formulation and a new name by an American State Department official, George F. Kennan. In an article published in 1947 in the journal *Foreign Affairs*, Kennan described what came to be known as the policy of "containment." It was based on the premise that the Soviet Union believed that communism would ultimately triumph, and that, therefore, the Soviets would not risk war if faced with resolute opposition. Thus, the main element in the policy of the United States "must be that of a long-term, patient but firm and vigilant containment of Russian expansive tendencies." The Russians must be confronted "with unalterable counterforce at every point where they show signs of encroaching upon the interests of a peaceful and stable world."

Practicing containment proved to be expensive both in terms of money and lives. In some areas, such as Western Europe, its application involved economic and military alliances and was successful. However, when communism expanded into Asia with the revolution in China in 1949, new threats arose. Applying containment in that part of the world led to the involvement of the United States in a costly war in Korea, and ultimately Vietnam.

Meanwhile, fears of communism spreading abroad provided the setting for another "Red Scare" at home. Recall that even prior to the Cold War, the American people occasionally had been alarmed about anarchists, socialists, and communists. Now the stakes seemed even higher due in part to the nuclear arms race which accompanied the Cold War. Spurred by the tactics and rhetoric of Senator Joseph McCarthy, the nation seemed willing to deny civil liberties to anyone accused of communist ties. While Senator McCarthy would lose credibility and his tactics were eventually condemned, communism remained as the dominant issue on the international scene.

In retrospect, the fifteen years after the end of World War II were much more unsettling in the area of foreign affairs than most Americans might have anticipated. The United States had taken up the burden of leadership for those countries resisting communism. The leader paid a heavy price, but significant gains were recorded. Western Europe had been largely restored to economic and political stability. Moreover, despite the spread of communism into China, South Korea stood as a symbol of the determination of the United States to maintain its commitment to resist aggression.

The emergence of the Soviet Union as a superpower nearly equal to the United States forced a reassessment of some aspects of American foreign policy. However, the concept of containment would continue to provide the framework for American policymakers, and the costs of being a world power would continue to be high as the world moved into the decade of the 1960s.

LEARNING OBJECTIVES

Goal—The purpose of this lesson is to increase our understanding of the efforts of the United States to contain the expansion of communism and the consequences of those actions both internationally and domestically.

Objectives—Upon completing this lesson, you should be able to:
1. Describe and explain the origins of the Cold War.
2. Describe and explain the development of the containment policy and how it was applied in Europe.
3. Analyze U.S. policy decisions in Asia, the Middle East, and Latin America in the context of the Cold War.
4. Assess the relationship of the Cold War and decisions made regarding nuclear weapons.
5. Analyze the effects of the Cold War on American society.

TEXT FOCUS POINTS

The following questions are designed to help you get the most from your reading. Review them before you do your reading. After completing the assignment, write responses and/or notes to reinforce what you have learned.

Text: Nash et al., *The American People*, Chapter 27, pp. 874-895.

1. Describe and explain the conflicting aims of the United States and the Soviet Union at the end of World War II.
2. Compare and contrast the leadership styles and world views of Presidents Truman and Eisenhower. How would you describe their Soviet counterparts?
3. What factors contributed to the emerging Cold War in 1945-1946?
4. How did George Kennan define the concept of containment? What was the significance of that concept?
5. How did the Truman Doctrine, Marshall Plan, Berlin airlift, NATO, and NSC-68 illustrate the application of the containment policy? Why did John Foster Dulles criticize containment?
6. Why and how did the United States engage in the Korean War? Why did President Truman dismiss General Douglas MacArthur? What were the consequences of the Korean War?
7. How did the actions of the United States in Iran and Latin America illustrate Cold War diplomacy?
8. What role did nuclear weapons play in the Cold War? What were the views of John Foster Dulles on the use of those weapons?
9. Describe Red Scare activities within the United States in the late 1940s and early 1950s.
10. How and why did Senator Joseph McCarthy emerge as the leader of the domestic Red Scare? How did McCarthy and the entire anti-communist crusade affect the country?

READER FOCUS POINTS

Reader: *Perspectives on America*, *Volume 2*, "Leaving for Korea," by Brady.

1. Why did the author join the Marines? How did his training to become an officer change him?
2. How did Mr. Brady describe his experiences from the time he went on active duty until his departure for Korea?

VIDEO FOCUS POINTS

The following questions are designed to help you get the most from the video segment of this lesson. Review them before you watch the video. After viewing the video segment, write responses and/or notes to reinforce what you have learned.

Video: "The Cold War Begins"

1. Why did the wartime alliance between the United States and the Soviet Union break down so quickly after World War II?
2. Why and how did the United States apply the containment policy in Europe? What were the effects of practicing containment there?
3. How did President Truman view the Korean War? Why and how was it a limited war?
4. What explains the rise and fall of Senator Joseph McCarthy and the Red Scare of the 1950s? What were the long-term effects of the Red Scare?
5. In summary, what were the costs and benefits of the Cold War?

ENRICHMENT IDEAS

These activities are not required unless your instructor assigns them. They are offered as suggestions to help you learn more about the material presented in this lesson.

1. Read and analyze the "Recovering the Past" segment on pages 900-901 of *The American People.* Write a report on that segment in which you answer the questions presented in the text.
2. Interview a veteran of the Korean War. Find out how the war affected the life of the veteran. After the interview, write a report in which you describe your findings and assess the significance of the Korean War on individual lives and on the nation.

SUGGESTED READINGS

See the "Recommended Reading" listings on pages 909-910 of the text if you wish to explore further the material presented in this lesson.

SUGGESTED WEB SITES

Several places in the textbook will include information marked "The History Place." This is a reference to a related web site. See the "Suggested Web Sites" at the end of the chapter of the textbook if you wish to further explore the material presented in this lesson.

PRACTICE TEST

The following items will help you evaluate your understanding of this lesson. Use the answer key at the end of the lesson to check your answers or to locate material related in each question.

MULTIPLE-CHOICE INSTRUCTIONS

Choose the single best answer. If more than one answer is required, it will be so indicated.

1. The Cold War resulted from
    A. Soviet but not American actions.
    B. isolationist attitudes across American society.
    C. differing expectations about the post-World War II world.
    D. incompetent leadership in the postwar world.

2. As leader of the Soviet Union at the end of World War II, Joseph Stalin believed that the
    A. capitalist system should be introduced inside Russia.
    B. best basis for governing the Soviet Union was a doctrine of fairness.
    C. United States should be trusted as an ally.
    D. Soviet Union must keep eastern Europe within its sphere of influence.

3. At the end of World War II, President Truman
    A. aided the Soviets in rebuilding their war-torn economy.
    B. continued lend-lease to the British but not the Soviets.
    C. ended the lend-lease program to all European nations.
    D. supported economic aid for the communist bloc countries.

4. The concept of containment became the basis for
    A. American foreign policy in the post-World War II period.
    B. unified support for revolutionary movements worldwide.
    C. Dean Acheson's claim to fame.
    D. stronger relations between the United States and the Soviet Union.

5. As enunciated by the president, the Truman Doctrine indicated that the United States would
   A. stay out of European affairs.
   B. protect Latin American countries from colonization.
   C. give aid to countries resisting communism.
   D. support nationalist revolutions in Asia.

6. During the Korean War, President Truman
   A. clearly stated the American objective to conquer North Korea.
   B. vigorously acted to oppose communist aggression.
   C. reluctantly cooperated with the United Nations' decision to defend South Korea.
   D. actively supported MacArthur's proposal to bomb communist bases in China.

7. In the Middle East during the Truman and Eisenhower administrations, the United States
   A. cooperated with the Soviets.
   B. protected Western access to Iranian oil supplies.
   C. refused to recognize the state of Israel.
   D. prevented Egypt from taking control of the Suez Canal.

8. In an attempt to deal with the problem of nuclear proliferation after World War II, President Truman
   A. threatened to attack the Soviets if they developed a nuclear bomb.
   B. agreed with the Soviet plan for control of nuclear research.
   C. rejected the plan proposed by Dean Acheson and David Lilienthal.
   D. eventually abandoned plans for international arms control.

9. In reaction to Cold War tensions, Congress
   A. called for negotiations between the Soviet Union and the United States.
   B. condemned President Truman's loyalty program as too severe.
   C. protected the civil rights of those accused of disloyalty.
   D. restricted Communist party activity in the United States.

10. During the second Red Scare, which developed during the 1950s,
    A. W. E. B. Du Bois defended the American way of life.
    B. the right of due process for those accused was often ignored.
    C. academics suffered few restrictions on freedom of speech.
    D. labor unions were generally unaffected.

11. James Brady, the author of "Leaving for Korea," joined the Marines because he
    A. came from a military family.
    B. dropped out of college.
    C. did not want to be drafted.
    D. wanted to escape the ghetto.

12. On the eve of his departure for Korea, author James Brady had feelings of
    A. fear and inadequacy.
    B. sadness and disappointment.
    C. frustration and anger.
    D. all of the above.

13. The wartime alliance between the United States and the Soviet Union broke down immediately after World War II for all of the following reasons EXCEPT
    A. competing economic systems.
    B. differing political philosophies.
    C. developing fears of the other side's motives.
    D. rejecting China's membership in the United Nations.

14. The Marshall Plan did all of the following EXCEPT
    A. revitalize the Western European economy.
    B. aid Communist Bloc countries.
    C. assure Western Europe of American support.
    D. develop markets for goods produced in the United States.

15. Senator Joseph McCarthy emerged as a leader of the Red Scare of the 1950s because he
    A. obtained evidence that the nation was overrun by subversives.
    B. expected labor unions to endorse communists in the 1948 elections.
    C. resisted the loyalty oath program of the Truman administration.
    D. needed a popular political issue.

16. One effect of the Cold War was that the United States
    A. consistently promoted political freedom overseas.
    B. often supported right-wing dictatorships.
    C. gradually reduced military expenditures.
    D. eventually withdrew from collective security pacts.

ESSAY/PROBLEM QUESTIONS

17. Describe and explain the development of the containment policy of the United States and analyze the application of that policy by the United States from 1945 to 1954.

18. Describe and explain the development of the Red Scare which took place in the United States in the late 1940s and early 1950s. What explains Senator Joseph McCarthy's role during this era? Why did the Red Scare diminish by the mid-1950s? What did the American people learn from this whole episode?

ANSWER KEY

Answers	Learning Objectives	Focus Points	References
1. C	1	T1, V1	Nash, pp. 874-876 and Video
2. D	1	T2	Nash, pp. 874-876
3. C	1	T3	Nash, p. 878
4. A	2	T4	Nash, pp. 878-879
5. C	2	T5, V2	Nash, pp. 878-879 and Video
6. B	3	T6, V3	Nash, p. 884 and Video
7. B	3	T7	Nash, pp. 885-887
8. D	4	T8	Nash, pp. 887-888
9. D	5	T9	Nash, pp. 891-892
10. B	5	T10	Nash, pp. 893-895
11. C	5	R1	Reader
12. A	5	R2	Reader
13. D	1	V1	Video
14. B	2	V2	Video
15. D	5	V4	Video
16. B	5	V5	Video
17.	All	All	Text, Reader, and Video
18.	All	All	Text, Reader, and Video

Lesson 18

An Age of Conformity

LESSON ASSIGNMENTS

Review the following assignments in order to schedule your time appropriately. Pay careful attention; the titles and numbers of the textbook chapter, the telecourse guide lesson, and the video program may be different from one another.

Text: Nash et al., *The American People, Volume Two: From 1865*,
            Chapter 26, "Postwar Growth and Social Change," pp. 838-871;
            Chapter 28, "High Water and Ebb Tide of the Liberal State," pp. 912-920;
            and Chapter 29, "The Struggle for Social Reform," pp. 946-951.

Video: "An Age of Conformity,"
            from the series *America in Perspective.*

OVERVIEW

The consensus which characterized the major policy decisions of the United States during the early Cold War era was also evident in many aspects of domestic life. At first, an understandable sense of euphoria swept the nation at the end of World War II in 1945. That generation of American people had faced the nation's most severe economic depression in the 1930s and then had won a difficult and costly war against truly frightening enemies. They were confident, optimistic, hard-working, and ambitious. They were ready "to settle down" and enjoy life, which very well might have meant a new suburban home, a new car, a television, and, by the end of the 1950s, taking the family to McDonald's for a hamburger. Historian William O'Neill offers this perspective:

> Delayed and disrupted by the war, members of this generation
> wanted to go back, even beyond their parents, to a time of secure
> values and traditional practices. They succeeded remarkably well,
> creating large, stable suburban families despite very high rates of

physical mobility. . . . Inward looking in one sense, it was generous otherwise in its emphasis on community, cooperation, and sharing. . . . The American High in large measure arose from satisfaction over gains that were very real, if not always permanent or without hidden costs. (*American High: The Years of Confidence, 1945-1960,* New York: FreePress, 1986, p. 44)

The "postwar economic boom" was fueled at first by wartime savings and then by a significant rise in real purchasing power. More discretionary income was available, and most Americans chose to spend it. Government policies helped focus some of the spending. The Servicemen's Readjustment Act of 1944 (GI Bill), called by Professor O'Neill "one of the brightest things Congress ever did," directed benefits toward education and housing. In addition, federal spending on major projects like the interstate highway system provided an economic boost and supported an ever-widening influence of the automobile on the American economy and society. Technological advances made the television affordable for more Americans, and computers even began to appear. Availability of consumer credit made it easy to buy new and improved products.

For the most part, union workers joined the middle class during the postwar years. Meanwhile, the growth of service-oriented jobs and the relative decline of "blue-collar" jobs began to erode the traditional base of union membership. In the corporate and agricultural segments of the American economy, the century-long trend toward bigness continued. Corporate mergers resulted in huge conglomerates and multinational operations. Farmers, aided by new chemical fertilizers and sprays and the use of more powerful machinery, continued to increase their productivity. The irony of American agriculture continued, as in many ways farmers produced themselves out of business, and thousands of farmers and/or the children of farmers went to the city for economic and social opportunities.

Although we know that not everyone shared in the general economic prosperity, a high degree of conformity characterized life in the 1950s. It seemed as though the vast majority of Americans were content to pursue their dreams in the booming suburbs. Life in these suburban communities, like the houses, became routine—but most people seemed to prefer it that way. A rising birth rate and a declining death rate led to a significant increase in population, which was now more than ever shifting to the Southwest and West. Even though more women than ever before entered the peacetime work force, there appeared to be a reassertion of the "woman's role" as wife-mother-homemaker. Meanwhile, men often put on the company uniform, even if that was a business suit, went to work outside the home, and complied with the company rules.

Politically, the era was marked by the presidencies of the Democrat Harry S. Truman (1945-1953) and the Republican Dwight D. Eisenhower (1953-1961). Truman's years were much more unsettling than Eisenhower's, particularly in reference to foreign policy crises, the initial adjustments to a peacetime economy, and his sometimes stormy relationship with Congress. In hindsight, what stands out was his willingness to take on the tough issues and make decisions. His dogged determination was rewarded by the voters in 1948 when he was elected in one of the biggest upsets in American presidential politics.

Unlike Truman, Eisenhower enjoyed tremendous popularity throughout his presidency. He seemed to be the right person for the times. For the most part, people did not want bold new leadership and confrontational politics. In some ways, Eisenhower may have disappointed the conservative Republicans by refusing to dismantle the New Deal. He was smart enough to realize that there was broad popular support for many of the governmental programs. Although he was certainly more "pro-business" than his predecessor, he had no intention of foolishly trying to take the nation back to the days of Calvin Coolidge and Herbert Hoover. Most historians consider Eisenhower, like Truman, to have been a better-than-average president.

While there were signs of "cultural rebellion" against the uniformity of the 1950s, minorities, particularly African Americans, presented an even more serious challenge to the status quo. While racial barriers were coming down in sports and the armed forces, in 1947 a presidentially appointed Committee on Civil Rights urged the federal government to move forward to secure the rights of all Americans. In 1954, the Supreme Court took a major step in that direction with its *Brown v. Board of Education* decision. Declaring that "separate but equal" schools were unconstitutional, the court signaled that racial segregation would eventually end. Of course, it would take years of struggle to rid society of segregation, but at least that struggle showed significant progress in the 1950s.

To place domestic life during the period 1945-1960 in perspective, we need to acknowledge its accomplishments and to understand its limitations. There was much that was good about the era, including an improved standard of living, better housing and education, and a sense of security for many Americans. Likewise, social evils did exist, including racism, sexism, and poverty. It was a significant time of transition between the tumultuous events which came before and afterward. It was also a significant time of growth and development which affected the American people and nation for the rest of the century.

LEARNING OBJECTIVES

Goal—The purpose of this lesson is to increase our understanding of domestic life in the late 1940s and 1950s and to assess the long-term significance of that era.

Objectives—Upon completion of this lesson, you should be able to:
1. Describe and explain the reasons for the general economic prosperity of the era and the effects of that prosperity.
2. Examine the effects of the GI Bill on American society.
3. Examine the social/cultural conformity of the era.
4. Analyze the reasons for the general political consensus on domestic issues and the effects of that consensus.
5. Describe and explain the conditions of minorities during the period and how and why they were challenging the status quo.

TEXT FOCUS POINTS

The following questions are designed to help you get the most from your reading. Review them before you do your reading. After completing the assignment, write responses and/or notes to reinforce what you have learned.

Text: Nash et al., *The American People*, Chapter 26, pp. 838-871; Chapter 28, pp. 912-920; and Chapter 29, pp. 946-951.

1. What factors explain the postwar economic boom?
2. How and why did the corporate world, the blue-collar workers' world, and the agricultural world change during the 1945-1960 period?
3. What were the general population trends of the era? How did the work of William J. Levitt capitalize on those trends?
4. How did major developments in technology affect American life during this time? What marketing trends encouraged consumption?
5. What characterized conformity and consensus in American life in the 1950s, especially for women? Who challenged the conformity, and what forms did the challenges take in literature, music, and art?
6. What were the major issues of the Truman administration, and what was his postwar public policy? What resistance did Truman's public policy receive?

Why did Harry Truman win the presidential election of 1948? After the election, what hindered his Fair Deal public policy?

7. What was Eisenhower's stand on the role of the government in economic matters and public welfare?

8. What factors contributed to greater national interest in civil rights in the late 1940s and 1950s?

9. What was the significance of the *Brown v. Board of Education* decision and the integration of Central High School in Little Rock, Arkansas? How and why did African Americans make gains on other fronts?

10. In what ways did the lives of Mexican Americans change during the 1945-1960 period? What limited improvement in their lives?

VIDEO FOCUS POINTS

The following questions are designed to help you get the most from the video segment of this lesson. Review them before you watch the video. After viewing the video segment, write responses and/or notes to reinforce what you have learned.

Video: "An Age of Conformity"

1. To what extent does the stereotypical image of life in America in the late 1940s and 1950s match reality? What were the positive and negative aspects of that era?

2. What factors explain the relative economic prosperity of the nation during the era?

3. What was the purpose of the GI Bill after World War II? How did that legislation affect American society?

4. Why did President Dwight Eisenhower and most Republicans accept the basic tenets of the New Deal?

5. What was the importance of the *Brown v. Board of Education* decision, the integration of Central High School in Little Rock, and the Montgomery bus boycott?

ENRICHMENT IDEAS

These activities are not required unless your instructor assigns them. They are offered as suggestions to help you learn more about the material presented in this lesson.

1. Read and analyze the "Recovering the Past" segment on pages 860-861 of *The American People*. Then write a 750-word essay in which you analyze how clothing styles reflected the times and answer the questions presented in the text.
2. If one or both of your parents grew up in the 1950s, interview them in order to gain insight on your own family history as well as the era. Then write a 750-word essay in which you describe how their lives reflected the times and how that experience affected the rest of their lives.
3. Read J. D. Salinger's *Catcher in the Rye* or Ralph Ellison's *Invisible Man*. Then write a book report in which you analyze what the novel says about the search for purpose and direction in life.
4. Read the article entitled "Inventing the Commercial" in *Perspectives on America, Volume 2*. Then write a 750-word essay in which you summarize the article and analyze the effects of television advertising on the American people.
5. Read the "Technology Changes the American People" segment about air conditioning on pages 852-853 of your textbook. Write a 750-word essay discussing the questions at the end of the text.

SUGGESTED READINGS

See the "Recommended Reading" listings on page 870 and pages 943-944 of the textbook if you wish to explore further the material presented in this lesson.

SUGGESTED WEB SITES

Several places in the textbook will include information marked "The History Place." These are references to related web sites. See the "Suggested Web Sites" at the end of the chapters in the textbook if you wish to further explore the material presented in this lesson.

PRACTICE TEST

The following items will help you evaluate your understanding of this lesson. Use the answer key at the end of the lesson to check your answers or to locate material related in each question.

MULTIPLE-CHOICE INSTRUCTIONS

Choose the single best answer. If more than one answer is required, it will be so indicated.

1. During the Eisenhower administration, material development of the United States was promoted by
   A. control of the economy by the Office of Price Administration.
   B. population shifts away from suburban areas.
   C. construction of the interstate highway system.
   D. less corporate control of the American economy.

2. By 1956, the majority of workers in the United States worked in
   A. factory jobs.
   B. white-collar jobs.
   C. self-employed jobs.
   D. agricultural jobs.

3. In the years since World War II, the American population has increasingly
   A. shifted away from the West and Southwest.
   B. concentrated poor nonwhites in the center of cities.
   C. rejected suburban living.
   D. insisted on less standard housing.

4. During the 1950s, material consumption in the United States was generally
   A. uninfluenced by advertising.
   B. inhibited by low salaries.
   C. limited due to the unavailability of luxury goods.
   D. facilitated by installment plans.

5. For women in the United States, the 1950s was a period when
   A. widespread resistance to traditional roles existed.
   B. male attitudes toward women's roles significantly changed.
   C. fewer married women worked.
   D. social pressure to fill traditional roles was great.

6. In terms of economic goals during his administration, President Truman attempted to
   A. restrict the policies of the New Deal.
   B. reduce government interference in the economy.
   C. guarantee full employment through government action.
   D. resist the liberal policies of the Republicans.

7. Truman's Fair Deal program
   A. suffered because of his preoccupation with the Cold War.
   B. promised gains for a select few in American society.
   C. received strong support of Congress.
   D. achieved overwhelming success.

8. It was Eisenhower's perception that government should
   A. expand the role of the president.
   B. grow to meet the needs of the nation.
   C. promote conservative fiscal policies.
   D. encourage economic activism.

9. All of the following factors contributed to greater national interest in civil rights during the late 1940s and 1950s EXCEPT
   A. increasing demands by minorities for change.
   B. growing political strength of minorities.
   C. rapid desegregation of public schools.
   D. America's position as leader of the "free world."

10. In response to the desegregation crisis at Central High School in Little Rock, Arkansas, President Eisenhower
   A. called out federal troops to protect black citizens.
   B. stated that laws were the best way to improve race relations.
   C. supported the position of the governor of Arkansas.
   D. privately endorsed desegregation while condemning it publicly.

11. During the 1950s, Mexican Americans
    A. continued to remain politically passive.
    B. faced little discrimination, unlike blacks.
    C. increasingly protested discriminatory treatment.
    D. effectively united their various protest movements.

12. The stereotypical image of suburban living in the 1950s was a
    A. reflection of the desires of increasing numbers of Americans.
    B. reality only for those in the top five percent of income.
    C. fabrication of popular writers of the times.
    D. dehumanizing myth for American women.

13. One key to post-World War II prosperity was
    A. continuing wage and price controls.
    B. spending of wartime savings.
    C. passing the Taft-Hartley Act.
    D. planning for the transition to peacetime economy.

14. The GI Bill directed that
    A. cash bonuses be paid.
    B. veterans' pensions be substituted for Social Security.
    C. benefits be targeted for housing and education.
    D. all-volunteer armed forces be created.

15. President Dwight Eisenhower and most Republicans accepted the basic tenets
    of the New Deal because they
    A. feared a communist takeover.
    B. converted to a liberal philosophy.
    C. abused social spending.
    D. realized that most programs worked.

16. One effect of the *Brown v. Board of Education* decision was to
    A. inspire challenges to other aspects of segregation.
    B. bring about immediate integration.
    C. ruin the public school system in America.
    D. prohibit teachers from striking.

ESSAY/PROBLEM QUESTION

17. Describe and explain the general economic conditions, the political consensus, and the social/cultural conformity of the 1950s. Who was challenging the conformity of the era, and how successful were their challenges? What is the long-term significance of the era in American life?

ANSWER KEY

	Answers	Learning Objectives	Focus Points	References
1.	C	1	T1	Nash, pp. 841-843
2.	B	1	T2	Nash, pp. 842-845
3.	B	1	T3	Nash, p. 848
4.	D	1	T4	Nash, pp. 855-857
5.	D	3	T5	Nash, pp. 858-859 and p. 862; Video
6.	C	1	T6	Nash, pp. 914-915
7.	A	4	T6	Nash, pp. 916-917
8.	C	4	T7	Nash, p. 918
9.	C	5	T8	Nash, pp. 948-950
10.	A	5	T9, V5	Nash, pp. 949-950 and Video
11.	C	5	T10	Nash, pp. 866-868
12.	A	3	V1	Video
13.	B	1	V2	Video
14.	C	2	V3	Video
15.	D	4	V4	Video
16.	A	5	V5	Video
17.		All	All	Text and Video

Lesson 19

Toward the American Dream

LESSON ASSIGNMENTS

Review the following assignments in order to schedule your time appropriately. Pay careful attention; the titles and numbers of the textbook chapter, the telecourse guide lesson, and the video program may be different from one another.

Text: Nash et al., *The American People, Volume Two: From 1865*,
           Chapter 28, "High Water and Ebb Tide of the Liberal State," pp. 912-914,
           pp. 920-921, pp. 924-932; and
           Chapter 29, "The Struggle for Social Reform," pp. 951-955.

Reader: *Perspectives on America, Volume 2*,
           "The Week the World Watched Selma," by Stephen B. Oates.

Video: "Toward the American Dream,"
           from the series *America in Perspective*.

OVERVIEW

As we have seen, the conformity which characterized the 1950s was not comfortable for all Americans. Minorities especially had not shared equally in the apparent affluence. African Americans in particular had led the challenge to the status quo, and they had achieved significant gains with the *Brown v. Board of Education* decision by the Supreme Court and the success of the Montgomery, Alabama, bus boycott.

      The winds of change sweeping the country picked up velocity in the presidential election year of 1960. John F. Kennedy's narrow victory brought to the White House a new sense of energy and exuberance. He appealed to people's better instincts and called for social justice. However, Kennedy's rhetoric on civil rights was better than his record. Limited by a conservative coalition in Congress and perhaps by his own lack of a deep personal commitment, President Kennedy moved slowly on civil rights issues until the spring of 1963. One thing that he had done prior to that year was to appoint federal judges who were sympathetic to the cause of civil rights. Those judges, along with Kennedy's successor, Lyndon Baines Johnson, would be extremely important to the cause of civil rights for the rest of the decade.

Meanwhile, black protest escalated. Sit-ins at lunch counters, freedom rides across the South, and mass demonstrations of both whites and blacks pushed the civil rights agenda forward. Most of these protests adhered to the philosophy of nonviolence espoused ever more eloquently by Martin Luther King, Jr. Nevertheless, violence often erupted. Resistance to the movement was led by reactionaries who were not about to change their habits and institutions without a fight. Most obviously in the South at this time, local and state authorities attempted to hold the line on discrimination and denial of equality.

A turning point came in Birmingham, Alabama, in April 1963. Considered "the most segregated city in the United States" by civil rights leaders, Birmingham presented a real challenge to the cause of integration. Violence erupted and protest leaders were arrested. Television coverage showed the nation the cruelty of the police and created a good deal of sympathy for the protesters among thoughtful viewers.

Furthermore, the Kennedy administration felt compelled to intervene to help end the violence and work out settlements of local grievances. More importantly, President Kennedy now broke his public silence on civil rights and spoke to the nation about the constitutional and moral imperative to move forward toward a more equal society. Within a matter of days, the administration sent to Congress a proposed civil rights bill which would prohibit discrimination in public places and extend voting rights.

The following summer was highlighted by a massive march on Washington, D.C., to bring additional pressure on Congress to pass civil rights legislation. The march culminated with King's "I Have a Dream" speech. King's words still remind us of how far we have come and how far we have to go to realize his vision.

After President Kennedy's tragic assassination in November 1963, President Lyndon Johnson moved quickly to push the civil rights bill through Congress. The Civil Rights Act of 1964, similar in many respects to an act that the Supreme Court had declared unconstitutional in 1883, was extremely important in breaking down long-established barriers to equality. During the next year, Johnson, aided by national publicity generated during the Selma-to-Montgomery march, pressured Congress to support legislation to help guarantee the right to vote to all qualified citizens. The result, the Voting Rights Act of 1965, became another landmark piece of legislation.

Meanwhile, President Johnson also moved forward with other aspects of his Great Society programs. Declaring a "war on poverty," he initiated a number of proposals which made it into the federal statutes during the next two years. Perhaps most significantly, health care provisions were added to the basic welfare system. It became popular in the 1970s and 1980s to pronounce the war on poverty a failure and to dismiss it as another misguided liberal attempt to aid the downtrodden. In fact, poverty did diminish during LBJ's presidency, and many of the initiatives of his administration are still in place three decades later. What derailed the war on poverty in the short term was primarily the escalating war in Vietnam. What still inhibits a full-scale attack on poverty is a lack of general will and moral commitment on the part of the American people to do so.

In retrospect, we can now see that the civil rights movement was entering a new phase by the end of 1965. Much had been accomplished, but the immediate tangible gains did not satisfy the expectations of many. New leaders were emerging to challenge King's philosophy and his goals. King himself was ready to move on to the North and to the issues of economic empowerment. At the same time, other minorities intensified their own efforts to move further toward the American Dream.

LEARNING OBJECTIVES

Goal—The purpose of this lesson is to increase our understanding of the civil rights movement of the early 1960s.

Objectives—Upon the completing this lesson, you should be able to:
1. Examine the political trends of the early 1960s.
2. Analyze the leadership and the tactics of the civil rights movement in the effort to bring about change.
3. Analyze the role of President Lyndon Johnson in furthering civil rights legislation and the effectiveness of his Great Society programs.
4. Assess the civil rights movement as of 1965.

The following questions are designed to help you get the most from your reading. Review them before you do your reading. After completing the assignment, write responses and/or notes to reinforce what your have learned.

Text: Nash et al., *The American People,* Chapter 28, pp. 912-914, pp. 920-921, pp. 924-932; and Chapter 29, pp. 951-955.

1. In what ways did the presidential election of 1960 dramatize the new trends in American politics and government? Why did John F. Kennedy win that election?
2. What were JFK's strengths as president? What factors limited his success?
3. What were Lyndon B. Johnson's strengths as president?
4. What were the major accomplishments of LBJ's Great Society? How did the Great Society compare with the reforms of the progressive era and the New Deal? What factors limited the success of the Great Society programs?
5. How did the major decisions of the Supreme Court in the early 1960s affect American society?
6. What tactics were used by civil rights activists in the early 1960s? What were the results of the protests?
7. What factors limited President Kennedy's initial responses to demands for civil rights? What moved him to a more aggressive approach? How did President Johnson respond to the civil rights movement?
8. What were the primary goals of Martin Luther King, Jr., during this era? What approach did he take in order to accomplish his goals?
9. What was the significance of the Civil Rights Act of 1964 and the Voting Rights Act of 1965?

READER FOCUS POINTS

Reader: *Perspectives on America, Volume 2,* "The Week the World Watched Selma," by Oates.

1. Why was Selma, Alabama, chosen as the site for a voting rights action in 1965? Why were the tactics of nonviolent protest so effective in this situation?
2. What was the significance of the Selma-to-Montgomery march?

VIDEO FOCUS POINTS

The following questions are designed to help you get the most from the video segment of this lesson. Review them before you watch the video. After viewing the video segment, write responses and/or notes to reinforce what you have learned.

Video: "Toward the American Dream"

1. What effect did the Kennedy administration have on the civil rights movement of the early 1960s?
2. Why did Martin Luther King, Jr., gain leadership in the civil rights movement?
3. What was the importance of the protest marches in Birmingham in 1963?
4. Why did President Lyndon B. Johnson push forward on civil rights and poverty programs? What changes came about during his presidency? How successful was the Great Society?
5. What had been accomplished by the civil rights movement as of 1965? What do those accomplishments teach us about the process of social change?

ENRICHMENT IDEAS

These activities are not required unless your instructor assigns them. They are offered as suggestions to help you learn more about the material presented in this lesson.

1. Read and analyze the "Recovering the Past" segment on pages 922-923 of *The American People*. Then write an essay in which you answer the questions presented in the text.
2. Interview someone who was active in the African American civil rights movement of the early 1960s. Using the interview as a primary source and reflecting upon what you have learned in this lesson, write a 750-word essay in which you analyze how the civil rights movement brought about change in America.
3. Read the article entitled "My Search for Lyndon Johnson" in *Perspectives on America, Volume 2*. Then write a 750-word essay in which you summarize the article and present your evaluation of LBJ's strengths and weaknesses.

SUGGESTED READINGS

See the "Recommended Reading" listings on pages 943-944 and pages 980-981 of the text if you wish to explore further the material presented in this lesson.

SUGGESTED WEB SITES

Several places in the textbook will include information marked "The History Place." These are references to related web sites. See the "Suggested Web Sites" at the end of the chapters in the textbook if you wish to further explore the material presented in this lesson.

PRACTICE TEST

The following items will help you evaluate your understanding of this lesson. Use the answer key at the end of the lesson to check your answers or to locate material related in each question.

MULTIPLE-CHOICE INSTRUCTIONS

Choose the single best answer. If more than one answer is required, it will be so indicated.

1. By the 1960s, most Americans tended to believe that the federal government should
   A. reduce its commitment to social welfare programs.
   B. abandon the philosophies of the New Deal and Fair Deal.
   C. radically reduce defense spending.
   D. assume a more active role in American society.

2. The inauguration of John Kennedy as president of the United States
   A. brought vigorous leadership to the government.
   B. continued Eisenhower's presidential leadership style.
   C. meant that Washington social life became less glamorous.
   D. led to an administration dominated by Roman Catholic values.

---

3. Presidents John Kennedy and Lyndon Johnson were similar in their
   A. culture and sophistication.
   B. ability to deal effectively with Congress.
   C. upbringing in families with great wealth.
   D. aggressive use of presidential power.

4. The most significant additions made by the Great Society to the reforms of the progressive era and the New Deal concerned
   A. medical care and civil rights.
   B. tax reform and business regulation.
   C. unemployment insurance and work programs.
   D. conservation and education.

5. The Supreme Court in the 1960s
   A. supported and promoted social changes.
   B. provided ineffective leadership.
   C. affirmed a conservative philosophy.
   D. restricted civil liberties.

6. When James Meredith applied for admission to the University of Mississippi in 1962,
   A. the state's governor supported him.
   B. riots resulted.
   C. the Supreme Court refused to support him.
   D. blacks boycotted the bus system in Oxford.

7. President John F. Kennedy became more assertive in advocating civil rights after
   A. sit-ins took place at lunch counters.
   B. Martin Luther King, Jr.'s, "I Have a Dream" speech.
   C. widespread violence in Birmingham, Alabama.
   D. southern congressmen urged him to do so.

8. Martin Luther King, Jr.'s, goal during the 1960s was to
   A. destroy the inequities of segregation.
   B. gain political office.
   C. win converts to his religion.
   D. promote racial violence.

9. The Civil Rights Act of 1964 was significant in that it
   A. prohibited segregated public schools.
   B. outlawed racial discrimination in all public accommodations.
   C. established the Civil Rights Commission.
   D. ordered the integration of the armed forces.

10. Martin Luther King, Jr., used the tactic of nonviolent protest because it
    A. required less organization than other methods.
    B. assured him of prominence in the movement.
    C. removed the threat of going to jail.
    D. allowed protesters to maintain moral principles.

11. Perhaps President John F. Kennedy's most significant effect on civil rights occurred through his
    A. support for forced busing.
    B. order to desegregate the armed forces.
    C. appointments to the federal courts.
    D. ability to appease conservative Democrats.

12. In the video program, Professor Darlene Clark Hine described one of Martin Luther King, Jr.'s, greatest attributes as his ability to
    A. organize protest demonstrations.
    B. mobilize people to act.
    C. initiate legislation in Congress.
    D. persuade presidents to fund special projects.

13. During LBJ's presidency, all of the following occurred EXCEPT
    A. civil rights protection.
    B. voting rights safeguards.
    C. outlawing segregated schools.
    D. extension of poverty programs.

14. Regarding change in America, the civil rights movement illustrated that
    A. social legislation does not influence people.
    B. violent protest is essential.
    C. collective action of ordinary people can make a difference.
    D. media attention is unimportant.

ESSAY/PROBLEM QUESTION

15. How and why was significant civil rights and other social legislation enacted during the mid-1960s? What was the short-term and the long-term significance of that legislation? What does that era teach us about change in America?

ANSWER KEY

Answers	Learning Objectives	Focus Points	References
1. D	1	T1	Nash, p. 920
2. A	1	T2	Nash, p. 921
3. D	3	T3	Nash, p. 926
4. A	3	T4	Nash, pp. 927-929
5. A	1	T5	Nash, pp. 929-930
6. B	2	T6	Nash, p. 953
7. C	2	T7, V3	Nash, pp. 953-955 and Video
8. A	2	T8, R2	Nash, pp. 951-953 and Reader
9. B	4	T9	Nash, p. 955
10. D	2	R1	Reader
11. C	1	V1	Video
12. B	2	V2	Video
13. C	3	V4	Video
14. C	4	V5	Video
15.	All	All	Text, Reader, and Video

Lesson 20

Expanding the American Dream

LESSON ASSIGNMENTS

Review the following assignments in order to schedule your time appropriately. Pay careful attention; the titles and numbers of the textbook chapter, the telecourse guide lesson, and the video program may be different from one another.

Text: Nash et al., *The American People, Volume Two: From 1865,* Chapter 29, "The Struggle for Social Reform," pp. 955-981.

Video: "Expanding the American Dream," from the series *America in Perspective.*

OVERVIEW

From one perspective, important changes had come about in the lives of African Americans between the *Brown v. Board of Education* decision in 1954 and the passage of the Voting Rights Act of 1965. Not only had legal segregation of public schools been prohibited and the political system made more accessible for blacks, but also significant progress had been made in knocking down legal discrimination in transportation, housing, and public accommodations.

From another perspective, real independence and equality for African Americans meant more than court decisions and federal laws. New and more strident voices pressed demands for economic empowerment and attacked a system they believed was still riddled with racism. Malcolm X, Stokely Carmichael, Huey Newton, and H. Rap Brown tended to frighten whites, but they did have an appeal to certain segments of the black community. Even Martin Luther King, Jr., became more outspoken regarding economic exploitation and racism.

Meanwhile, in the mid-1960s riots broke out in many of the nation's major cities. The tragedy of this violence was compounded with the assassinations of Martin Luther King, Jr., and Robert F. Kennedy in 1968. The chaotic demonstrations outside the Democratic party convention that summer contributed to the election of the Republican presidential candidate, Richard M. Nixon, who promised to restore law and order. The Nixon administration may well have reflected a majority opinion of white Americans when it took measures to slow down progress in the civil rights movement. The majority may have been willing to grant equal political and legal rights in the 1960s and early 1970s, but economic equality was another matter.

African Americans were not the only minority attempting to expand the American Dream. Hispanic Americans, particularly Mexican Americans, historically had faced race and class discrimination similar to blacks. Their success in overturning legal segregation in public schools predated similar advances by African Americans. In the 1960s and 1970s, Cesar Chavez led a direct challenge to the economic plight of large numbers of Mexican Americans. Other Mexican American leaders emerged to press for more equal treatment on other fronts.

Organized protest by women against unequal treatment dates back to the Seneca Falls Convention and its Declaration of Sentiments in 1848. The primary focus of women activists in the late nineteenth and early twentieth centuries had been the vote. Once accomplished, organized feminism went into decline. The "liberation" of the 1920s was symbolized by the playful flapper. Then came the Great Depression and World War II. After the war, the emphasis seemed to be on home and family, with the woman expected to be wife-mother-homemaker.

It was that expectation, both real and psychological, that Betty Friedan critiqued in her 1963 book, *The Feminine Mystique*. Friedan basically called for women to be able to exercise options that were commonly open to men. In order for that to happen, women would have to become more assertive regarding their civil rights. The timing of the book obviously coincided with the increasingly vocal protests of the black civil rights movement. Women activists would pick up on the tactics of that movement, and the fact that some of them had faced personal discrimination within that movement only increased their determination. Even though organized feminists of the era failed to gain ratification of the Equal Rights Amendment, the most blatant forms of sex discrimination began to crumble. Women pursued higher education and entered the workforce in unprecedented numbers, although their earning power remained considerably less on the average than their male counterparts.

American Indians were also more assertive regarding their rights in the 1960s and 1970s. They sought redress in court for treaty violations, engaged in occasional militant and well-publicized protest demonstrations, and demanded a greater degree of self-determination. Although many American Indians remained in dire poverty, the actions taken by them and on their behalf during that era provided a reference point for moderate improvement in some conditions in the years since.

Not all of those seeking change in the 1960s and 1970s were necessarily members of an identifiable minority group. Perhaps most significantly in the long term, the contemporary environmental and consumer movements came out of that era. In addition, it was a time when large numbers of college students appeared to challenge the attitudes and beliefs of their elders. Underscoring this generation gap was a counterculture which often shocked the establishment. Much of this disillusionment expressed by the youth of the era had to do with the Vietnam War and the Watergate affair, events which we will analyze more closely in subsequent lessons.

At the time, the era of the 1960s and the early 1970s appeared to be a wildly exciting time to some and a threat to others. Opportunities opened up, and traditional values and ways of doing things were questioned. In retrospect, it remains a fascinating period for analyzing change in America. Causes, leadership, organization, public support—elements came together to move the nation in a different direction. The political, legal, and even cultural changes of that era were real but, as is usually the case in America, relatively slow and moderate in their effects. The economic changes some had hoped for generally stalled, and they remain to be addressed by those who still want to expand the American Dream.

LEARNING OBJECTIVES

Goal—The purpose of this lesson is to increase our understanding of efforts by minority groups and others in the late 1960s and 1970s to expand and perhaps redefine the American Dream.

Objectives—Upon completing this lesson, you should be able to:
1. Describe and explain why the African American civil rights movement seemed to splinter in the mid-1960s and then to stall by the mid-1970s.
2. Analyze the emergence and the success of the Hispanic, women's, and American Indian protest movements.
3. Analyze the emergence and the effects of the social and cultural protest indicated by the student movement, counterculture trends, and the environmental and consumer movements.
4. Assess the changes that had taken place in America as a result of the whole civil rights movement and the other social and cultural movements of the era.

TEXT FOCUS POINTS

The following questions are designed to help you get the most from your reading. Review them before you do your reading. After completing the assignment, write responses and/or notes to reinforce what you have learned.

Text: Nash et al., *The American People,* Chapter 29, pp. 955-981.

1. How did Malcolm X, Stokely Carmichael, Huey Newton, and H. Rap Brown challenge the leadership of Martin Luther King, Jr.? How did the riots in American cities in the mid-1960s represent additional challenges to liberal reform?

2. What actions did President Nixon and the Republican party take to slow down the black civil rights movement? Why was busing such a controversial issue? Describe and explain the gains and losses for African Americans during the 1970s.

3. What factors gave rise to the women's movement? What were the major goals of the movement?

4. Who opposed the women's movement? What limited its success?

5. Describe the status of Hispanic Americans in the 1960s and 1970s. How did Cesar Chavez help improve the lives of Mexican Americans?

6. In addition to Chavez, what other leaders and organizations sought to change the status of Mexican Americans? What did they accomplish? What limited progress for Hispanic Americans?

7. What were the goals and accomplishments of the American Indian protest movement?

8. What factors explain the student movement? What were the major issues addressed by this movement?

9. What characterized the counterculture? What were some of the results from the emphasis on personal fulfillment?

10. What gave rise to the environmental and consumer movements? What resulted from these efforts?

VIDEO FOCUS POINTS

The following questions are designed to help you get the most from the video segment of this lesson. Review them before you watch the video. After viewing the video segment, write responses and/or notes to reinforce what you have learned.

Video: "Expanding the American Dream"

1. Why did the black civil rights movement splinter after 1965? Why did urban riots break out in the mid-1960s? What were the effects of the riots and violent protests? What is Julian Bond's opinion about violent protest in America?
2. What victories had been achieved in the area of civil rights by Mexican Americans prior to the 1960s? What was Cesar Chavez's role in the struggle to improve economic conditions for Mexican Americans? How did the Voting Rights Act of 1965 affect Mexican Americans?
3. Why did the women's rights movement emerge in the 1960s? Why did the Equal Rights Amendment fail to win ratification? What changes did take place for women during this era?
4. Why did the civil rights movement stall by the mid-1970s?
5. What does the whole civil rights movement teach us about change in America?

ENRICHMENT IDEAS

These activities are not required unless your instructor assigns them. They are offered as suggestions to help you learn more about the material presented in this lesson.

1. Interview someone who was active in the women's, Hispanic, or American Indian protest movement of the 1960s and 1970s. Using the interview as a primary source and reflecting upon what you have learned in this lesson, write a 750-word essay in which you analyze how one of these movements brought about change in America.
2. If your parents are of the appropriate age, interview one or both of them about how the social and cultural movements of the 1960s and 1970s affected their lives. Using that interview as a primary source to supplement what you have learned in this lesson, write a 750-word essay in which you analyze how that era affected your family and American society in general.

3. Read and analyze the "Recovering the Past" section of *The American People* text on pages 976-977. Then write a 750-word report in which you answer the questions presented in the text.

SUGGESTED READINGS

See the "Recommended Reading" listings on pages 980-981 of the text if you wish to explore further the material presented in this lesson.

SUGGESTED WEB SITES

Several places in the textbook will include information marked "The History Place." This is a reference to a related web site. See the "Suggested Web Sites" at the end of the chapter of the textbook if you wish to further explore the material presented in this lesson.

PRACTICE TEST

The following items will help you evaluate your understanding of this lesson. Use the answer key at the end of the lesson to check your answers or to locate material related in each question.

MULTIPLE-CHOICE INSTRUCTIONS

Choose the single best answer. If more than one answer is required, it will be so indicated.

1. In general, by the mid-1960s Malcolm X, Stokely Carmichael, Huey Newton, and H. Rap Brown
   A. accepted the basic tenets of capitalism.
   B. rejected nonviolent protest as the best way to help blacks.
   C. agreed to work closely with Martin Luther King, Jr.
   D. refused to endorse the concept of "black power."

2. The use of busing as a means for desegregation of American schools often
   A. eliminated de facto but not de jure segregation.
   B. caused violent resistance when white students were involved.
   C. gained acceptance by southern whites without protest.
   D. received endorsement from President Nixon.

3. The founders of the National Organization of Women contended that women, in general,
   A. gained equal opportunity from the Civil Rights Act of 1964.
   B. received unequal treatment as members of society.
   C. perceived consciousness-raising as unimportant.
   D. approved of traditional marriage relationships.

4. During the 1970s, the women's movement in the United States
   A. continued to experience internal divisions.
   B. achieved ratification of the Equal Rights Amendment.
   C. evolved into a unified organization.
   D. generated little support for women's causes.

5. Prior to the 1970s, Hispanic Americans were
   A. unwilling to share the American Dream.
   B. often culturally and economically separated from the rest of society.
   C. greatly helped by Great Society programs.
   D. unsuccessful in gaining a political voice.

6. As leaders among Mexican Americans during the 1960s and 1970s, Rodolfo "Corky" Gonzáles, Reis López Tijerina, and José Angel Gutiérrez did all of the following EXCEPT
   A. press for return of land taken from Mexicans years earlier.
   B. participate in political protest movements.
   C. support the war in Vietnam with enthusiasm.
   D. engage in confrontational activities with the authorities.

7. As a result of activities by the American Indians during the 1960s and 1970s, the
   A. general population became less sympathetic to Indian causes.
   B. presidential administrations encouraged termination of reservations.
   C. culture and fashions of American Indians became more popular.
   D. Indian leaders rejected all attempts to improve reservation life through capitalism.

8. An important factor in explaining the student protest movements of the 1970s was the
   A. decline in college enrollment.
   B. depressed condition of the American economy.
   C. population decline.
   D. increasing educational opportunity.

9. The activities of the countercultural youth in the 1960s and 1970s revealed
   A. social polarization within American society.
   B. commitment to law and order by the counterculture.
   C. acceptance of Nixon's foreign policy.
   D. interest in the American political process.

10. During the 1960s and 1970s, the environmental movement was successful in all of the following efforts EXCEPT
    A. lobbying for passage of environmental legislation.
    B. increasing public awareness of environmental dangers.
    C. gaining the support of conservative state legislators for strict enforcement of environmental regulations.
    D. linking environmental improvements to the popular desire for a better "quality of life."

11. Urban riots and violence associated with black protests after 1965 brought about
    A. lessening of white support.
    B. new civil rights initiatives in Congress.
    C. success for Democrats in the 1968 presidential election.
    D. widespread endorsement of affirmative action programs.

12. Prior to the 1960s, Mexican Americans had obtained court rulings which
    A. assured income levels equal to Anglos.
    B. restored lost landholdings.
    C. ordered bilingual education.
    D. promised desegregated schools.

13. A women's rights movement emerged in the 1960s for all of the following reasons EXCEPT
    A. publication of *The Feminine Mystique*.
    B. experience by women activists in the black civil rights movement.
    C. realization that legislation could help women.
    D. passage of the Equal Rights Amendment.

14. The black civil rights movement stalled when its leaders
    A. demanded significant economic changes.
    B. suggested a coalition with other minorities.
    C. failed to produce capable replacements.
    D. argued against the Equal Rights Amendment.

15. To bring about change, the civil rights movement taught Americans that
    A. violent protest must be sustained.
    B. organizational work is essential.
    C. revolution is necessary.
    D. stirring speeches are useless.

ESSAY/PROBLEM QUESTION

16. Compare and contrast the black, women's, Hispanic, and American Indian protest movements during the era from 1965 to the mid-1970s. In general, what do these and other movements of that era illustrate about change in America?

ANSWER KEY

Answers	Learning Objectives	Focus Points	References
1. 1	1	T1	Nash, pp. 955-958
2. B	1	T2	Nash, pp. 958-959
3. B	3	T3	Nash, p. 960-961
4. A	2	T4	Nash, pp. 961-964
5. B	2	T5	Nash, p. 964
6. C	2	T6	Nash, p. 966
7. C	2	T7	Nash, pp. 968-969
8. D	3	T8	Nash, p. 970
9. A	3	T9	Nash, pp. 972-974
10. C	3	T10	Nash, pp. 974-975 and pp. 978-979
11. A	1	V1	Video
12. D	2	V2	Video
13. D	2	V3	Video
14. A	4	V4	Video
15. B	4	V5	Video
16.	All	All	Text and Video

Lesson 21

The Limits of Power: Vietnam

LESSON ASSIGNMENTS

Review the following assignments in order to schedule your time appropriately. Pay careful attention; the titles and numbers of the textbook chapter, the telecourse guide lesson, and the video program may be different from one another.

Text: Nash et al., *The American People, Volume Two: From 1865,*
             Chapter 27, "Chills and Fever During the Cold War," pp. 895-910.

Reader: *Perspectives on America, Volume 2,*
             "Vietnam: The War That Won't Go Away," by George Herring

Video: "The Limits of Power: Vietnam,"
             from the series *America in Perspective.*

OVERVIEW

On a cold January 20, 1961, President John Fitzgerald Kennedy delivered a stirring inaugural address. Much of the speech had to do with the role of the United States in the world:

> . . . Let the word go forth from this time and place, to friend and foe alike, that the torch has been passed to a new generation of Americans—born in this century, tempered by war, disciplined by a hard and bitter peace, proud of our ancient heritage—and unwilling to witness or permit the slow undoing of those human rights to which this nation has always been committed, and to which we are committed today at home and around the world.
>
> Let every nation know, whether it wishes us well or ill, that we shall pay any price, bear any burden, meet any hardship, support any

friend, oppose any foe . . . to assure the survival and the success of liberty.

These words, so moving in the context of the early 1960s, did not arouse the same reaction by the mid-1970s. By then a great many Americans had become quite disillusioned about their willingness to "pay any price, bear any burden, [and] meet any hardship" in world affairs. In some ways, perhaps it may have been analogous to the disillusionment of Americans of an earlier generation—those who listened to the uplifting oratory of President Woodrow Wilson only to be brought down by the harsh realities of a world war and its subsequent hardships. Likewise, the Vietnam War did much to destroy the buoyant optimism and confidence of the generation living half a century after Wilson.

As the 1960s opened, the Cold War was still raging and the United States was still committed to its policy of containment. That policy had been tested in Europe and in Asia in the late 1940s and during the 1950s at considerable cost, but on the whole, the United States was basically satisfied with the results. Now events in Cuba and in Vietnam presented new challenges to containment and to President Kennedy's pledge on behalf of the nation.

As we now know, the Cuban missile crisis brought the United States and the Soviet Union to the brink of nuclear war. That crisis occurred just eighteen months after the United States was involved in a failed attempt to overthrow Cuban leader Fidel Castro, who had taken that island nation into the communist camp. The confusion of the Bay of Pigs invasion raised doubts about the direction and decisiveness of President Kennedy's leadership. However, those doubts were largely dissipated by his firm stand against Soviet missiles in Cuba.

The confidence President Kennedy gained may have contributed to his willingness to commit to an escalation of American involvement in an ongoing conflict in Vietnam. Of course, we will never know what Kennedy's ultimate decisions regarding Vietnam would have been. We do know that President Lyndon Johnson authorized the major escalation of United States forces in Vietnam between 1965 and 1968. After Johnson left the presidency, a gradual reduction of American forces ordered by President Richard Nixon took place. However, the United States remained engaged in the war until a cease-fire agreement was reached in January 1973. Slightly more than two years later, South Vietnam was overrun by the communist forces of the North.

Beyond forcing a reassessment of the containment policy in Asia in the mid-1970s, the lessons of the Vietnam War are many. Studies published in recent years have attempted to put the war in perspective. One common theme which cuts across many of these analyses is that the United States did not understand what it was getting into until it was much too late. The general lack of knowledge by American policymakers regarding the commitment of the North Vietnamese, especially Ho Chi Minh and his followers, to national unity and to be free of foreign domination was fundamental to the American tragedy. The United States did not lose the war because of television or because of war protests or because the military did not fight hard enough. The United States lost because the majority of the American people decided that the war was not worth fighting any more. Those who did fight suffered enormously, and they did not seem to be appreciated—that too was one of the real tragedies of the war.

In the short term, the Vietnam War had significant political effects. Besides the political polarization which took place in the United States, many historians believe that the war contributed to President Nixon's demise. His obsession with leaks and punishment of political enemies, which became so crucial in the Watergate scandal, was apparent in his handling of wartime opposition. On an even broader scale, the war should have taught Americans that we need a rational national debate *before* committing ourselves to an overseas war against an enemy whom we do not understand.

George Herring, perhaps the foremost scholar on Vietnam, concludes that the impact on world politics of America's failure there "was considerably less than United States' policymakers had predicted." The war and subsequent events showed that the domino theory was a myth. Another historian, Paul Conway, has remarked that "now Vietnam is peripheral to American security interests, just as it was before the war." For years, the Vietnam syndrome seemed to affect decisions about American intervention overseas. By the 1980s and 1990s, however, American presidents and their advisers seemed anxious to reassert the power of the United States and prove once again that America was ready to try to police the world.

LEARNING OBJECTIVES

Goal—The purpose of this lesson is to increase our understanding of why the United States engaged in the Vietnam War and how that war affected the American people and policymakers.

Objectives—Upon completing this lesson, you should be able to:
1. Describe and explain the reasons for the involvement of the United States in Vietnam in the 1940s and 1950s.
2. Examine the factors which led to the escalation of U.S. military forces in Vietnam in the 1960s.
3. Analyze the factors which led to the eventual withdrawal of U.S. forces from Vietnam.
4. Assess the effects of the Vietnam War on American foreign policy as well as on domestic life.
5. Analyze the changing relationship of the United States with the Soviet Union and China in the early 1970s.

TEXT FOCUS POINTS

The following questions are designed to help you get the most from your reading. Review them before you do your reading. After completing the assignment, write responses and/or notes to reinforce what you have learned.

Text: Nash, *The American People,* Chapter 27, pp. 895-910.

1. What explains President Kennedy's actions regarding Cuba in 1961 and 1962? What were the results of the Cuban missile crisis?
2. Why did the United States get involved in Vietnam in the 1950s? What actions did the Eisenhower administration take regarding Vietnam?
3. Why and how did Presidents Kennedy and Johnson escalate the involvement of the United States in Vietnam? What was the significance of the Gulf of Tonkin resolution in the process of escalation?
4. What was the importance of the Tet offensive, My Lai, Kent State, and the *Pentagon Papers* on the course of the war and/or the American perception of it?
5. What was President Nixon's policy regarding the Vietnam War? What were the costs of the Vietnam War?

6. Why did the Nixon administration pursue the policy of "détente" regarding the Soviet Union and China? What were the results of that policy?

READER FOCUS POINTS

Reader: *Perspectives on America, Volume II,* "Vietnam: The War That Won't Go Away." by Herring.

1. Why was the Tet offensive a turning point in the Vietnam War?
2. Why did the Vietnam War lead to so much divisiveness at home?
3. Why was the Vietnam War such a difficult war to fight for American soldiers?
4. Why did President Johnson continue to pursue the war? Why did President Nixon? How is the war linked to the Watergate scandal?

VIDEO FOCUS POINTS

The following questions are designed to help you get the most from the video segment of this lesson. Review them before you watch the video. After viewing the video segment, write responses and/or notes to reinforce what you have learned.

Video: "The Limits of Power: Vietnam"

1. How did the outcome of the Cuban missile crisis affect American policy toward Vietnam?
2. Why did the United States get involved in Vietnam prior to the 1960s? How did American actions there run counter to the nation's traditions? Why was the failure to hold elections in Vietnam in 1956 so important?
3. How did the war protest movement and media coverage of the Vietnam War affect political leaders and the outcome of the war?
4. How did the Vietnam War affect domestic life in America?
5. How did the Vietnam War affect American attitudes toward foreign intervention? What did the United States learn from its experience in Vietnam?

ENRICHMENT IDEAS

These activities are not required unless your instructor assigns them. They are offered as suggestions to help you learn more about the material presented in this lesson.

1. Interview someone who is a veteran of the Vietnam War. Using that interview as a primary source and reflecting upon what you have learned in this lesson, write a 750-word essay in which you analyze the effects of the Vietnam War on individuals, families, and the nation as a whole.
2. Read the book, *America's Longest War,* by George Herring. Then write a 750-word review in which you critically analyze the main themes of the book.
3. Read and analyze the "Recovering the Past" section of *The American People* text on pages 900-901. Then write a 750-word report in which you answer the questions presented in the text.

SUGGESTED READINGS

See the "Recommended Reading" listings on page 909-910 of the text if you wish to explore further the material presented in this lesson.

SUGGESTED WEB SITES

Several places in the textbook will include information marked "The History Place." This is a reference to a related web site. See the "Suggested Web Sites" at the end of the chapter of the textbook if you wish to further explore the material presented in this lesson.

The following items will help you evaluate your understanding of this lesson. Use the answer key at the end of the lesson to check your answers or to locate material related in each question.

MULTIPLE-CHOICE INSTRUCTIONS

Choose the single best answer. If more than one answer is required, it will be so indicated.

1. All of the following resulted from the Cuban missile crisis EXCEPT
   A. emergence of President Kennedy as a hero.
   B. establishment of a direct Soviet-American telephone line.
   C. removal of American nuclear missiles from NATO forces.
   D. Soviet determination to increase its nuclear arsenal.

2. At the end of World War II, the United States became involved in Vietnam because
   A. it was part of the larger Cold War against the Soviet Union.
   B. Ho Chi Minh had fought as an ally of Japan during the war.
   C. an international trusteeship for the area was not working.
   D. U.N. forces needed help.

3. The Gulf of Tonkin resolution was significant because it indicated
   A. congressional approval for military action in Vietnam.
   B. loss of support in Congress for President Johnson.
   C. the need for opening peace talks in Vietnam.
   D. the approval of the United States of Diem's assassination.

4. As a result of the killing of students at the antiwar demonstration at Kent State University in 1970,
   A. a planned invasion of Cambodia was called off.
   B. the National Guard was brought under regular army command.
   C. more questions were asked about the use of troops at home and in Vietnam.
   D. the war protest movement lost its momentum.

5. Under President Richard Nixon, U.S. policy concerning the Vietnam War led to
   A. increased involvement of American ground troops.
   B. immediate decrease in American air attacks on North Vietnam.
   C. refusal by the United States to negotiate with the North Vietnamese.
   D. replacement of American troops with South Vietnamese troops.

6. The basic goal of the Nixon administration's policy of "détente" was to
   A. force France to defend itself.
   B. establish more cordial relations with China and the Soviet Union.
   C. secure North Vietnamese withdrawal from South Vietnam.
   D. form a closer working relationship with Latin American countries.

7. As a result of the Tet offensive,
   A. many Americans questioned U.S. policy in Vietnam.
   B. President Johnson gained in popularity.
   C. American forces withdrew from the countryside in Vietnam.
   D. American bombing of North Vietnam stopped.

8. The Vietnam War became divisive because
   A. people in America had little knowledge of what was going on.
   B. most Republicans opposed the war.
   C. threats to American security were not readily apparent.
   D. economic recession gripped the nation at home.

9. The Vietnam War was difficult for American soldiers because
   A. military equipment was outdated.
   B. guerilla fighting made it hard to distinguish the enemy.
   C. insufficient money was being spent.
   D. Vietnamese people became friends.

10. President Johnson escalated the Vietnam War for all of the following reasons EXCEPT his
   A. refusal to give up.
   B. commitment to success.
   C. inability to find a solution.
   D. disregard for American soldiers.

11. The outcome of the Cuban missile crisis resulted in
    A. confidence among policymakers which carried over to Vietnam.
    B. agreement to avoid use of nuclear weapons in Vietnam.
    C. North Vietnam attacking the South.
    D. Soviet withdrawal of forces from Vietnam.

12. The war protest movement
    A. caused President Nixon to cease bombing North Vietnam.
    B. received funding and leadership from the communists.
    C. raised questions and increased divisions in society.
    D. resulted in no effect on the outcome of the Vietnam War.

13. At home, the Vietnam War
    A. contributed to the defeat of President Nixon in 1972.
    B. received little media attention.
    C. created a renewed sense of national unity.
    D. helped bring on the economic crises of the 1970s.

14. One lesson of Vietnam is that
    A. Congress will not support an undeclared war.
    B. press censorship during wartime is essential.
    C. foreign intervention must be grounded in domestic support.
    D. America should remove all military forces from Asia.

ESSAY/PROBLEM QUESTION

15. Describe and explain why the United States became involved in the Vietnam War, how that war affected American society, and why the United States eventually withdrew its military forces. What were some of the major conclusions drawn from that war?

ANSWER KEY

Answers	Learning Objectives	Focus Points	References
1. C	2	T1	Nash, pp. 896-897
2. A	1	T2, V2	Nash, p. 897 and Video
3. A	2	T3	Nash, pp. 899 and 902
4. C	3	T4	Nash, pp. 902-904
5. D	3	T5	Nash, pp. 903-904
6. B	5	T6	Nash, pp. 905-907
7. A	3	R1	Reader
8. C	4	R2	Reader
9. B	4	R3	Reader
10. D	2	R4	Reader
11. A	2	V1	Video
12. C	3	V3	Video
13. D	4	V4	Video
14. C	4	V5	Video
15.	All	All	Text, Reader, and Video

Lesson 22

The Limits of Politics

LESSON ASSIGNMENTS

Review the following assignments in order to schedule your time appropriately. Pay careful attention; the titles and numbers of the textbook chapter, the telecourse guide lesson, and the video program may be different from one another.

Text: Nash et al., *The American People, Volume Two: From 1865,*
Chapter 28, "High Water and Ebb Tide of the Liberal State,"
pp. 932-941.

Reader: *Perspectives on America, Volume 2,*
"I Am Not a Crook! Corruption in Presidential Politics," by Kenneth G. Alfers.

Video: "The Limits of Politics,"
from the series *America in Perspective.*

OVERVIEW

The Vietnam War not only challenged the limits of American power, but also aroused skepticism regarding American political leadership. Much of this skepticism was directed at the president, for the power of the chief executive had taken on unprecedented dimensions after World War II. Presidential power had also expanded in order to maintain "law and order" at home in the face of spreading violence. Did the "imperial president" have any limits?

    While the concept of the imperial presidency is most associated with historian Arthur M. Schlesinger, Jr., the fear of a too-powerful chief executive has been around since the Constitution was written. The framers of the Constitution had recognized the danger and had shrewdly constructed an elaborate system of checks and balances to assure that none of the three branches of the central government could exercise unlimited power. The term *imperial presidency*, according to

Schlesinger, "refers to the condition that ensues when the constitutional balance between presidential power and presidential accountability is upset in favor of presidential power." (*The Imperial Presidency*, Boston: Houghton Mifflin, 1973, p. 420.)

World War II not only solidified the pervasive role of the federal government in the lives of the American people, but also it transformed the United States into a permanent world power. It was in this context of the United States as superpower, with ominous enemies emerging during the Cold War, that the imperial presidency began to threaten the constitutional balance of power. By the time Richard Nixon became president in 1969, the office had taken on many of the trappings of a monarch. The combination of that trend and Nixon's personality led to a constitutional crisis.

> Historically Congress had maintained the rough balance of the Constitution because it retained three vital powers: the war-making power, the power of the purse, and the power of oversight and investigation. By 1950 it had relinquished the war-making power. Truman fought in Korea, Johnson in Vietnam, and Nixon in Cambodia without the explicit congressional authorization required by the Constitution. From 1969 to 1974, the Nixon administration tried systematically and, until Watergate, successfully to nullify the other two powers: countering the power of the purse by the doctrine of unlimited impoundment of appropriated funds; countering the power of oversight by the doctrine of unreviewable executive privilege and the extension of the presidential secrecy system. Had Nixon succeeded in imposing these doctrines on top of his amplified claims for the presidential war-making power, he would have effectively ended Congress as a serious partner in the constitutional order.
>
> His further contribution to the imperial presidency was to take emergency powers the presidency had accumulated in order to save the republic from foreign adversaries and to turn these powers against his political opponents—"enemies," he called them—at home. Invoking "national security" as an all-purpose justification for presidential criminality, he set up a secret White House posse to burgle offices; forge historical documents;and wiretap officials, embassies, newspapermen, and "enemies." The presidency was above the law, and national crisis justified extreme methods. (*The Imperial Presidency*, pp. 421-422.)

The exposure of the Watergate scandal is a fascinating tale which illustrates the corruption of the Nixon administration as well as the workings of the checks and balances system. The courts, Congress, and the free press all worked to bring criminals to justice and to rein in a president who had misused and abused power.

The significance of the whole Watergate scandal needs to be considered in the full perspective of American political history. This was more than a case of a few corrupt politicians who happened to get caught. Nixon and his cohorts went beyond the corruption of the Grant and Harding administrations. Since Nixon left office, only the Reagan administration has approached the level of corruption revealed in the early 1970s.

One conclusion that should *not* be drawn from the Watergate scandal, even though it is popular to do so, is that it merely confirms the notion that "all politicians are crooks." As students of history, we must base our conclusions on *evidence*. To do otherwise is to engage in mere fantasy and unwarranted speculation. It is not fair to brand all politicians as crooks simply because the Nixon administration was full of them; likewise, it is not just to excuse Richard Nixon by falsely claiming that he was no worse than the average politician.

LEARNING OBJECTIVES

Goal—The purpose of this lesson is to increase our understanding of the rise and fall of the imperial presidency during the administration of Richard Nixon.

Objectives—Upon completing this lesson, you should be able to:
1. Analyze Richard Nixon's election victory in 1968, his administrative style, and the domestic policies of the Nixon administration.
2. Describe and explain the development of the imperial presidency.
3. Examine the factors which led to the development and the exposure of the Watergate scandal, culminating in the resignation of Richard Nixon.
4. Assess the immediate and long-term effects of the Watergate scandal in particular and political corruption in general.

TEXT FOCUS POINTS

The following questions are designed to help you get the most from your reading. Review them before you do your reading. After completing the assignment, write responses and/or notes to reinforce what you have learned.

Text: Nash et al., *The American People,* Chapter 28, pp. 932-941.

1. What factors explain Richard Nixon's victory in the presidential election of 1968?
2. Describe Richard Nixon's personality and administrative style.
3. What were the major economic issues facing the Nixon administration? How did President Nixon address those issues, including welfare reform?
4. Why did the Nixon administration emphasize "law and order" and how was it to be restored?
5. What factors explain the development of the Watergate scandal?
6. How and why was the Watergate scandal exposed? What factors led to President Nixon's resignation?
7. What characterized Gerald Ford's presidency?

READER FOCUS POINTS

Reader: *Perspectives on America, Volume 2,* "I Am Not a Crook! Corruption in Presidential Politics," by Alfers.

1. What were the similarities and differences of the Grant, Harding, and Nixon scandals?
2. Why was the Watergate scandal of the Nixon administration "the most centralized and pernicious of all"?
3. Why was political corruption rampant during the Reagan presidency?

VIDEO FOCUS POINTS

The following questions are designed to help you get the most from the video segment of this lesson. Review them before you watch the video. After viewing the video segment, write responses and/or notes to reinforce what you have learned.

Video: "The Limits of Politics"

1. What is meant by the term "imperial presidency"? Why did presidents assume more power in the mid-and late-twentieth century?
2. How had Richard Nixon's background and personality shaped his view of the presidency?
3. Why did the Watergate scandal unravel?
4. Why did Richard Nixon choose not to take decisive steps to rid his administration of scandal?
5. To what extent did the Watergate affair change politics? In the end, what was the significance of the Watergate scandal?

ENRICHMENT IDEA

This activity is not required unless your instructor assigns it. It is offered as a suggestion to help you learn more about the material presented in this lesson.

Read *The Imperial Presidency* by Arthur M. Schlesinger, Jr., or *The Final Days* by Bob Woodward and Carl Bernstein, and then write a 750-word critical analysis of the book.

SUGGESTED READING

See the "Recommended Reading" listings on pages 943-944 of the text if you wish to explore further the material presented in this lesson.

Several places in the textbook will include information marked "The History Place." This is a reference to a related web site. See the "Suggested Web Sites" at the end of the chapter of the textbook if you wish to further explore the material presented in this lesson.

PRACTICE TEST

The following items will help you evaluate your understanding of this lesson. Use the answer key at the end of the lesson to check your answers or to locate material related in each question.

MULTIPLE-CHOICE INSTRUCTIONS

Choose the single best answer. If more than one answer is required, it will be so indicated.

1. In running his administration, President Nixon preferred to
    A. work alone or with a few trusted advisers.
    B. use an open forum to arrive at decisions.
    C. seek advice regularly from Democratic congressional leaders.
    D. appoint minorities to key cabinet positions.

2. During the Nixon administration, the most critical factor which disrupted the American economy was the
    A. price of food.
    B. oil embargo.
    C. war in Vietnam.
    D. control of wages and prices.

3. All of the following were parts of President Nixon's attempts to restore "law and order" in the United States EXCEPT
    A. publicly denouncing demonstrators.
    B. using government power to alleviate the causes of crime.
    C. attacking the communications industry.
    D. appointing conservative judges to federal courts.

4. As Richard Nixon planned his reelection campaign in 1972,
   A. grave concern over the lack of campaign funds emerged.
   B. personnel seemed less organized than in 1968.
   C. sweeping the presidential and congressional elections became the Republican goal.
   D. conduct of a quiet and gentlemanly campaign seemed the best approach.

5. The effect of newspaper and televised reports of the Watergate scandal was to
   A. prove that liberals were out to get Nixon.
   B. cause an erosion of public support for President Nixon.
   C. prevent the reelection of President Nixon in 1972.
   D. cause the president to install a taping system in his office.

6. In comparing the Nixon and Ford presidencies,
   A. Nixon was much abler in developing a personable administration.
   B. both had little experience with the reins of power in Washington.
   C. both had popular mandates supporting their policies.
   D. Ford seemed to provide a reassuring presence in the White House.

7. The scandals associated with Grant, Harding, and Nixon are similar in all of the following ways EXCEPT
   A. occurrence during Republican administrations.
   B. initial denial of wrongdoing.
   C. expansion of presidential power prior to each administration.
   D. retirement from office richer than when they entered.

8. One particularly odious feature of the Watergate scandal involved
   A. press exposure of White House secrets.
   B. lies by the president and his aides.
   C. revelations of tape-recorded conversations.
   D. disloyalty of presidential aides.

9. One reason why political corruption was so rampant during the Reagan administration was the
   A. incompetence of presidential aides.
   B. liberal rulings by the Supreme Court.
   C. dominance of Republicans in Congress.
   D. president's administrative style.

10. In the video program, Arthur Schlesinger, Jr., maintained that the imperial presidency occurs when presidents
    A. engage in deficit spending.
    B. veto social legislation.
    C. exercise power without proper accountability.
    D. nominate friends to the Supreme Court.

11. In the video program, Professor Joan Hoff indicated that by the time of his presidency, Richard Nixon
    A. believed he had mastered the art of politics.
    B. acquired too many enemies to be effective.
    C. suffered from serious fits of depression.
    D. realized that Spiro Agnew was implicated in scandal.

12. In the video program, Professor Joan Hoff pointed out that Richard Nixon did not rid his administration of scandal partly because he was
    A. directly responsible for the Watergate break-in.
    B. innocent of any impropriety.
    C. not apprised of the seriousness of the issue.
    D. expecting to be pardoned for any criminal activity.

13. In retrospect, the Watergate affair
    A. failed to bring about significant political reform.
    B. damaged the press badly.
    C. demonstrated Nixon to be no more guilty than other presidents.
    D. illustrated the impracticality of the impeachment process.

ESSAY/PROBLEM QUESTION

14. Describe and explain the development and the exposure of the Watergate scandal. How did the corruption of the Nixon administration differ from that of other presidential administrations? What does the Watergate scandal teach us about the checks and balances system?

ANSWER KEY

Answers	Learning Objectives	Focus Points	References
1. A	1	T2	Nash, p. 934
2. B	1	T3	Nash, p. 935
3. B	1	T4	Nash, pp. 937-938
4. C	1	T5	Nash, pp. 939-940
5. B	3	T6, V3	Nash, pp. 939-940 and Video
6. D	4	T7	Nash, pp. 940-941
7. D	4	R1	Reader
8. B	4	R2	Reader
9. D	4	R3	Reader
10. C	2	V1	Video
11. A	2	V2	Video
12. C	3	V4	Video
13. A	4	V5	Video
14.	All	All	Text, Reader, and Video

Lesson 23

The Conservative Resurgence

LESSON ASSIGNMENTS

Review the following assignments in order to schedule your time appropriately. Pay careful attention; the titles and numbers of the textbook chapter, the telecourse guide lesson, and the video program may be different from one another.

Text: Nash et al., *The American People, Volume Two: From 1865*, Chapter 28, "High Water and Ebb Tide of the Liberal State," pp. 941-943 ("The Carter Interlude"); and Chapter 30, "The Revival of Conservatism," pp. 982-993.

Video: "The Conservative Resurgence," from the series *America in Perspective*.

OVERVIEW

Looking back, we can now see that the United States was ripe for a resurgence in conservative politics by the late 1970s. The previous fifteen years had been stressful times in all aspects of American life. The broad-based civil rights movement had challenged the status quo and initiated some significant changes affecting the lives of almost all Americans. The Vietnam War not only caused a reexamination of American commitments overseas, but also gave impetus to divisions at home. In addition, the Watergate affair had led to President Nixon's resignation and had furthered the skepticism, if not the increasing cynicism, of the American public regarding politicians and political institutions. In short, by 1976 there was a good deal of fear that "traditional" values and beliefs were eroding.

Jimmy Carter was able to capitalize on many of America's frustrations when he won the presidency in 1976. He took advantage of a backlash to the corruption associated with the Watergate affair, an event with which he had no connection (and his opponent, Gerald Ford, could not quite escape). Ironically, frustrations with

---

Carter's seeming inability to control foreign and domestic affairs would partially explain why he lost the presidency to Ronald Reagan in 1980.

While President Carter struggled, a conservative resurgence could be detected across the nation. It was most obvious in the growing middle-class suburbs, where resentment over high taxes, welfare programs, and bureaucratic regulations was strong. In addition, there was a growing public frustration with the general liberal reliance on government to help solve most of the nation's problems and with the increasing permissiveness in American society. Tax revolts and the rise of the Moral Majority indicated the shifting sentiments in the country. Meanwhile, conservative politicians began to master new and effective political techniques, including direct mail solicitation and television advertising. As one historian remarked, the conservatives were making their cause, for the first time since World War II, "intellectually respectable."

We can now see that by 1980 the stage was set for Ronald Reagan, perhaps the perfect candidate to capitalize on the conservative tide and the frustrations sweeping the country. Reagan appeared reasonable and likeable, and he offered simple solutions to complex problems. After all, when a candidate promises to lower taxes, increase military spending, and balance the budget all at the same time, it is quite tempting to support him. Besides, Reagan was an actor by profession, and he could use television to his advantage. Reagan was able to convince the majority of voters that most of the economic problems in America were the result of too much government interference. At the same time, he suggested that he favored the government's intervention in moral issues like abortion and school prayer. Rather than costing him the election, this apparent contradiction on the role of the government in American society reflected the conservative thinking of the time.

Once President Reagan was in office, he moved quickly to implement a large portion of the conservative agenda. During the first six months of his administration, a compliant Congress agreed to significant tax cuts, reductions in social spending, and increases in military appropriations. In many ways, the trickledown economics of the Coolidge era was revisited. David Stockman, President Reagan's first budget director, even admitted as much, although the Reaganites preferred, for obvious reasons, to call it "supply-side economics."

In addition to the tax and spending policies, the Reagan administration accelerated the movement to deregulate American businesses, a trend that began even during the Carter administration. Even when regulations remained on the statute books, enforcement of the laws was often deliberately neglected. Unregulated exploitation and materialism was in vogue. One historian described it as an attempt "to promote the public good through the pursuit of private wealth."

Another clear message coming out of the early stages of the Reagan administration was delivered when the nation's air traffic controllers went on strike during the summer of 1981. The president quickly fired the striking workers who, as government employees, technically did not have the right to strike. Reagan's actions went beyond breaking the union; the whole affair indicated that his administration would be more than sympathetic to management in any disputes with labor organizations.

Although the Reagan administration was successful in pushing most of its economic measures through Congress, it did not have as much success with its moral agenda. Although the president said he supported constitutional amendments which would protect public prayer in public schools and prohibit abortion, he did not press as hard on these issues as on his economic measures. Meanwhile, televangelists seemed omnipresent in the early 1980s, encouraging moral reform and contributions to their churches. Efforts of the evangelicals to refashion education through school prayer, creationism, and the spread of Christian academies reminded some historians of the fundamentalist crusades of the 1920s.

What were some of the political, economic, and social results of the conservative resurgence? At first, the country went through one its worst economic recessions during 1981-1982. When the economy recovered in 1983-1984, President Reagan was able to take credit as he sought reelection. However, the political realignment that many thought had been confirmed by the 1980 elections did not extend far beyond the presidential level. In economic terms, the rich ultimately benefited the most from the recovery and Reagan's economic policies. However, that fact was not yet clear by 1984. What was evident at that time was that the president's promise to balance the budget would not be kept. In another strange bit of inconsistency, the economic recovery was due in no small measure to deficit spending. Reagan, who had long condemned Keynesian economic policy, became its greatest practitioner! Were the people and the nation mortgaging their economic future through the enormous national, trade, and personal debts that began to emerge in the early 1980s? As the nation approached the 1984 elections, the majority of American voters were not yet ready to deal with such difficult long-term decisions.

LEARNING OBJECTIVES

Goal—The purpose of this lesson is to increase our understanding of the development and results of the conservative trend in American politics which occurred during the late 1970s and early 1980s.

Objectives—Upon completing this lesson, you should be able to:
1. Describe and explain the major economic trends of the era.
2. Analyze the electoral success of Jimmy Carter in 1976 as well as the domestic record of his administration.
3. Analyze the electoral successes of Ronald Reagan and George Bush in the 1980s and the political, economic, and social effects of their domestic program.
4. Analyze the electoral success of Bill Clinton in 1992 and 1996 and his administration.

TEXT FOCUS POINTS

The following questions are designed to help you get the most from your reading. Review them before you do your reading. After completing the assignment, write responses and/or notes to reinforce what you have learned.

Text: Nash et al., *The American People*, Chapter 28, pp. 941-943 ("The Carter Interlude"); and Chapter 30, pp. 982-993.

1. Why did Jimmy Carter win the 1976 presidential election? What explains his limitations on the domestic front?
2. What explains the appeal of conservative politics in the 1980s?
3. Why did Ronald Reagan win the 1980 and 1984 presidential elections? What characterized President Reagan's administrative style?
4. What changes did the Reagan administration initiate in the 1980s? What were the effects of these changes?
5. Why did Bill Clinton win the presidential elections of 1992 and 1996? Assess the major domestic initiatives of his administration.

VIDEO FOCUS POINTS

The following questions are designed to help you get the most from the video segment of this lesson. Review them before you watch the video. After viewing the video segment, write responses and/or notes to reinforce what you have learned.

Video: "The Conservative Resurgence"

1. What were Jimmy Carter's strengths as a presidential candidate in 1976? What were his weaknesses as a president?
2. What explains Ronald Reagan's appeal as a presidential candidate in 1980?
3. Why was there a conservative resurgence in 1980? To what extent did President Reagan implement the conservative agenda? What were the initial effects of this action?
4. How did the Reagan administration represent a turning point regarding the role of government in society? What problems emerged as a result of this transition?

ENRICHMENT IDEA

This activity is not required unless your instructor assigns it. It is offered as a suggestion to help you learn more about the material presented in this lesson.

> Interview someone who voted for Ronald Reagan in the 1980 and 1984 presidential elections. Try to determine what factors influenced that vote. Using the interview as a primary source and reflecting upon what you have learned in this lesson, write a 750-word essay in which you analyze those two presidential elections and what the results of that election signified about American politics at that time.

SUGGESTED READINGS

See the "Recommended Reading" listings on pages 943-944 and 1024-1025 of the text if you wish to explore further the material presented in this lesson.

SUGGESTED WEB SITES

Several places in the textbook will include information marked "The History Place." These are references to related web sites. See the "Suggested Web Sites" at the end of the chapters in the textbook if you wish to further explore the material presented in this lesson.

PRACTICE TEST

The following items will help you evaluate your understanding of this lesson. Use the answer key at the end of the lesson to check your answers or to locate material related in each question.

MULTIPLE-CHOICE INSTRUCTIONS

Choose the single best answer. If more than one answer is required, it will be so indicated.

1. President Jimmy Carter's effectiveness on the domestic front was hampered by his
    A. insistence on a balanced budget.
    B. proposals to nationalize energy sources.
    C. demand for tightening government regulation of business.
    D. perceived lack of clear direction for his programs.

2. During the 1980s, conservatives capitalized on changing political techniques in all of the following ways EXCEPT using
    A. brief "sound bites" to establish positions.
    B. open-ended press conferences to allow full discussion of the issues.
    C. negative ads to attack an opponent's character.
    D. enormous fund-raising to finance campaigns.

3. Ronald Reagan won the presidential election of 1980 partly because he
    A. seemed intellectually superior to Jimmy Carter.
    B. appeared more moderate than Jimmy Carter.
    C. presented himself well through the media.
    D. attracted a majority of black voters.

4. One of the chief results of President Reagan's administration was to
   A. reduce tensions with the Soviet Union.
   B. reduce federal spending on social programs.
   C. increase aid to the poor.
   D. aggressively defend minority rights.

5. Voters rejected President George Bush in the 1992 presidential election because most of them
   A. were disillusioned because of recent economic and social trends.
   B. thought the nation needed stronger leadership in foreign affairs.
   C. wanted Ross Perot to straighten out the mess in Washington.
   D. advocated a more conservative approach to the nation's problems.

6. Jimmy Carter won the presidency in 1976 largely because he
   A. articulated a sweeping reform program.
   B. demonstrated experience in foreign affairs.
   C. avoided association with the Washington establishment.
   D. possessed unusual intelligence.

7. The conservative resurgence reflected in Reagan's victory in 1980 was based on
   A. a growing need to restore ethics in government.
   B. a disillusionment with government.
   C. a desire to address environmental issues.
   D. concern for Soviet advances in Europe.

8. One effect of the electoral success of Ronald Reagan was to
   A. solve the nation's most pressing domestic problems.
   B. belittle the liberal approach to social ills.
   C. prove that less government was better for everyone.
   D. assure lower taxation for the rest of the century.

ESSAY/PROBLEM QUESTION

9. Describe and explain the development and the results of the conservative resurgence in American politics which occurred in the late 1970s and early 1980s.

ANSWER KEY

Answers	Learning Objectives	Focus Points	References
1. D	2	T1, V1	Nash, pp. 941-943 and Video
2. B	3	T2	Nash, pp. 984-986
3. C	3	T3, V2	Nash, pp. 986-987 and Video
4. B	3	T4	Nash, p. 989
5. A	4	T5	Nash, pp. 991-992
6. C	2	V1	Video
7. B	2	V3	Video
8. B	3	V4	Video
9.	All	All	Text and Video

Lesson 24

An Era of Excess

LESSON ASSIGNMENTS

Review the following assignments in order to schedule your time appropriately. Pay careful attention; the titles and numbers of the textbook chapter, the telecourse guide lesson, and the video program may be different from one another.

Text: Nash et al., *The American People, Volume Two: From 1865*,
            Chapter 30, "The Revival of Conservatism," pp. 994-1009, 1012-1014.

Reader: *Perspectives in America, Volume 2*,
            "Revolution in Indian Country," by Fergus M. Bordewich, and
            "Can We Still Afford to Be a Nation of Immigrants?," by David Kennedy.

Video: "An Era of Excess,"
            from the series *America in Perspective*.

OVERVIEW

As is so often the case in American history, presidential elections provide us with an opportunity to gauge public sentiment regarding national issues. In 1984, the voters had a clear choice: continue the policies of President Ronald Reagan or reject them in favor of the alternatives proposed by Democrat Walter Mondale. Since the nation had recovered from the severe recession of 1980-1982 and was at peace, it was not surprising that the majority of voters chose to extend Reagan's presidency for four more years.

It was during President Reagan's second term that excess became a characteristic of much of American society. Ironically, by the end of the decade, even greed had reached some limits. Just as the Great Society may have been limited by the government's attempts to do too much, the excessive materialism of the 1980s may have defined how far the majority of Americans were willing to allow pursuit of personal gain to go.

By the mid-1980s, greed seemed triumphant. Corporate mergers dominated the business news. Bigger was better, and corporate managers often lived in the fastest lane of all. Donald Trump became a hero to some, as he built monuments to himself and his opulent lifestyle was flashed across the society pages. The stock market followed suit, with stories of fabulous wealth accumulated by merely shuffling paper. Michael Milken, a stockbroker, reportedly had an income of more than $550 million a year! Banks and savings and loan institutions soon got in on the act: easy money was at hand. Even prominent religious leaders endorsed the trend and tried to cash in on it. Perhaps this was the final refinement of the Protestant work ethic that had always sanctioned the accumulation of riches as a sign of God's favor.

For those who had not yet cracked the upper echelon of wealth, the pattern for their lives was being set by the "yuppies." They came to symbolize the emphasis on self-centered materialism. They seemed most concerned with expensive cars, designer clothes, and careers. They were into physical fitness, psychic harmony, a tasteful lifestyle, and money. Author James Fixx made a fortune writing books about the virtues of running, until he dropped dead of a heart attack! Jane Fonda, an acclaimed actress and political radical of the 1960s and early 1970s, became a fitness guru by the mid-1980s. By 1987, a survey of college freshmen indicated that making money was their top goal in life.

By the late 1980s, a time of reckoning was at hand. Excess in all its ugliness was exposed in business, government, and religion. Donald Trump had trouble floating all of his debts. Michael Milken faced criminal punishment for illegal activities on the stock market. The market itself crashed in the fall of 1987. Banks began to fail with alarming regularity, and savings and loans soon followed. Meanwhile, most working-class Americans struggled to make economic ends meet. The decline in well-paid factory jobs marked a decade in which income distribution shifted significantly in favor of the rich.

As the 1980s progressed, exposures of political scandal surfaced. The Reagan administration's policies of deregulation and the detached style of the president himself contributed to one of the most scandal-ridden periods in our history. The mess at the Department of Housing and Urban Development was linked to financial irregularities found elsewhere. The blatant excess at the Pentagon illustrated the effects of throwing money at the military-industrial complex. Ethics in government, like business, seemed to be a joke. Some pundit coined the term "sleaze factor" to refer to the Reagan administration's "failure to comprehend ethics and outright scandals."

In times of low ethical standards, it would have been comforting if the American people could have turned to their religious leaders to provide guidance. Unfortunately, some of the most sensational scandals of the era involved highly recognizable religious leaders. The hypocrisy and greed of people like Jimmy Swaggart and Jim Bakker served as a commentary on the era.

While much of the nation's attention was focused on the lifestyles of the rich and famous, many of the nation's problems worsened. Perhaps most glaringly, race relations between whites and blacks seemed to regress. Reported overt racial incidents increased during the 1980s, and the Reagan administration gave clear signals that civil rights protection for minorities was not one of its high priorities. Cities struggled to deal with the homeless, illicit drug activity, and crime. The AIDS epidemic frightened almost everyone. Public education begged for meaningful reform, and the environment demanded attention.

The presidential election of 1988 hardly served as a forum for a debate and referendum on the future directions of the nation. Republican George Bush made elaborate promises about cleaning up the environment and becoming an "education" president, all the while guaranteeing no new taxes. The Republicans branded the Democratic nominee, Michael Dukakis, as a liberal, soft on black criminal rapists, and too inexperienced to deal with a changing world. It was an effective campaign, and Dukakis proved to be a weak opponent. Meanwhile, real proposals to deal with real issues were conveniently postponed.

Reflections on the 1980s bring to mind other eras in American history when the nation experienced an emphasis on materialism and excess. Parallels with the 1880s-1890s and the 1920s are most obvious, and some similarities with the 1950s can be noted. Each of those earlier periods was followed by times which tested the resiliency of the American people. Let us hope that once again the nation can draw upon its inner strength as it faces the challenges sure to arise at the beginning of a new century.

LEARNING OBJECTIVES

Goal—The purpose of this lesson is to increase our understanding of the costs and benefits of the economic, social, and political developments of the 1980s.

Objectives—Upon completing this lesson, you should be able to:
1. Describe and explain the major social trends of the 1980s and the early 1990s.
2. Analyze the costs and benefits of the economic, social, and political developments of the 1980s and the early 1990s.
3. Assess the trends of the 1980s and early 1990s in comparison to other eras.

TEXT FOCUS POINTS

The following questions are designed to help you get the most from your reading. Review them before you do your reading. After completing the assignment, write responses and/or notes to reinforce what you have learned.

Text: Nash et al., *The American People*, Chapter 30, pp. 994-1009, 1012-1014.

1. How and why did conditions change for minorities and for the environmental movement during the 1980s and 1990s?
2. What characterized the economic conditions during the 1980s and 1990s?
3. What characterized the population shifts in the United States during the 1980s? How did immigration patterns shift in the 1970s and 1980s? How did the new arrivals affect American society?
4. How and why did growing up and growing old change in the United States from the mid-1970s to the early 1990s? What effects did these changes have on American society? What did the Los Angeles riot of 1992 indicate about social conditions in the 1990s?

READER FOCUS POINTS

Reader: *Perspectives in America, Volume 2*, "Revolution in Indian Country," by Bordewich, and "Can We Still Afford to Be a Nation of Immigrants?," by Kennedy.

1. What have been the major effects of recent federal Indian policy?
2. What are the results of the tribal sovereignty movement? Why does the author favor an alternate approach?
3. What is novel about immigration to the United States in recent times? How is this immigration similar to that of earlier eras?
4. What makes immigration from Mexico different from traditional immigration?
5. How does Professor Kennedy answer the question posed at the beginning of his address? Why did he come to that conclusion?

VIDEO FOCUS POINTS

The following questions are designed to help you get the most from the video segment of this lesson. Review them before you watch the video. After viewing the video segment, write responses and/or notes to reinforce what you have learned.

Video: "An Era of Excess"

1. Why did Ronald Reagan win the 1984 presidential election?
2. What characterized the American economy during the 1980s? Who benefited and who lost economically? What role did President Reagan play in these economic developments?
3. Why was so little done to address social problems during the 1980s? When will these problems get addressed?
4. What are the consequences of a large federal deficit?
5. In what ways were the 1980s similar to other eras in American history? What do such comparisons teach us?

ENRICHMENT IDEA

This activity is not required unless your instructor assigns it. It is offered as a suggestion to help you place your own experiences in historical perspective.

> Read and analyze the "Recovering the Past" section of *The American People* text on pages 1010-1011. Then write your own autobiography, limiting yourself to 1,000 words.

SUGGESTED READINGS

See the "Recommended Reading" listings on pages 1024-1025 of the text if you wish to explore further the material presented in this lesson.

SUGGESTED WEB SITES

Several places in the textbook will include information marked "The History Place." This is a reference to a related web site. See the "Suggested Web Sites" at the end of the chapter of the textbook if you wish to further explore the material presented in this lesson.

PRACTICE TEST

The following items will help you evaluate your understanding of this lesson. Use the answer key at the end of the lesson to check your answers or to locate material related in each question.

MULTIPLE-CHOICE INSTRUCTIONS

Choose the single best answer. If more than one answer is required, it will be so indicated.

1. During the 1980s, all of the following were signs of regression in the areas of political and civil rights for African Americans EXCEPT
    A. presidential campaigns of Jesse Jackson in 1984 and 1988.
    B. backlash against affirmative action policies.
    C. court decisions supporting racial separation.
    D. presidential appointments to agencies enforcing civil rights.

2. All of the following factors contributed to economic stagnation in the United States in the early 1980s EXCEPT
    A. rising oil prices.
    B. aggressive foreign competition.
    C. too much research and development funding.
    D. declining industrial productivity.

3. Unlike earlier periods in American history, during the 1970s and 1980s, most immigrants to the United States came from
    A. Asia and Latin America.
    B. eastern and western Europe.
    C. Canada and northern Europe.
    D. Africa and Australia.

4. A significant characteristic of family life in the United States during the 1980s was an increase in the number of
    A. traditional families.
    B. children living with both parents.
    C. extended families sharing living quarters.
    D. divorces.

5. By the 1990s, a generation of legislation and court actions regarding the status of American Indians had
   A. canonized tribal autonomy.
   B. stripped them of civil rights.
   C. strengthened the Bureau of Indian Affairs.
   D. eroded their claims on mineral resources.

6. The American Indian tribal sovereignty movement has resulted in
   A. widespread support from state legislatures.
   B. tighter controls by the Bureau of Indian Affairs.
   C. efforts to nationalize mineral deposits on tribal lands.
   D. conflict with non-Indians who own property within tribal boundaries.

7. In the reading, Professor David Kennedy raised the possibility that
   A. American borders with Mexico could be closed.
   B. English could be constitutionally mandated in the United States.
   C. Mexican immigrants could form the basis of a semi-autonomous state in America.
   D. immigration quotas could be drastically reduced.

8. Economic studies conducted during the 1980s indicate that immigration
   A. causes a loss of economic opportunity.
   B. explains the economic recession of the early 1980s.
   C. relates very little to economic growth.
   D. contributes to economic vitality.

9. Ronald Reagan won the 1984 presidential election for all of the following reasons EXCEPT
   A. economic recovery had taken place.
   B. federal budgets were balanced.
   C. national defense seemed stronger.
   D. his personality was pleasing to most.

10. The people who benefited most from the economic developments of the 1980s were
    A. blue-collar workers.
    B. farmers.
    C. financiers.
    D. minorities.

11. In the video program, Professor William O'Neill stated his opinion that social problems receive adequate attention when
    A. Republicans control Congress.
    B. foreign intervention ceases.
    C. catastrophe forces action.
    D. federal budgets are balanced.

12. One consequence of a large federal deficit is that
    A. taxes can likely be lowered.
    B. cutbacks in vital expenditures can occur.
    C. wasteful spending can be totally eliminated.
    D. Republican economic policies can gain credibility.

13. The 1980s resembled the 1880s in the sense that both eras were times of
    A. enlightened political leadership.
    B. strong union movements.
    C. greed and selfishness.
    D. strict government regulation.

ESSAY/PROBLEM QUESTION

14. Describe and explain the costs and benefits of the major economic, social, and political developments of the 1980s and early 1990s. What did these developments portend for the rest of the decade?

ANSWER KEY

Answers	Learning Objectives	Focus Points	References
1. A	1	T1	Nash, pp. 994-995
2. C	2	T2	Nash, pp. 999-1000
3. A	1	T3,R3	Nash, pp. 1006-1008
4. D	1	T4	Nash, p. 1009
5. A	1	R1	Reader
6. D	1	R2	Reader
7. C	3	R4	Reader
8. D	2	R5	Reader
9. B	2	V1	Video
10. C	2	V2	Video
11. C	1	V3	Video
12. B	2	V4	Video
13. C	3	V5	Video
14.	All	All	Text, Reader, and Video

Lesson 25

The Cold War Ends

LESSON ASSIGNMENTS

Review the following assignments in order to schedule your time appropriately. Pay careful attention; the titles and numbers of the textbook chapter, the telecourse guide lesson, and the video program may be different from one another.

Text: Nash et al., *The American People, Volume Two: From 1865,* Chapter 30, "The Revival of Conservatism," pp. 1014-1026.

Video: "The Cold War Ends," from the series *America in Perspective.*

OVERVIEW

We have a particularly interesting vantage point from which to put American foreign policy in perspective. A little more than one hundred years ago, the United States was just preparing to reach out and exercise its emerging economic and military strength. From that time to this, the nation has played a vital role in shaping the course of world history. Events in the late 1980s and 1990s once again changed world power relationships and presented the United States with new challenges. One thing that will not change is the basic framework within which the American people and their leaders will continue to make their decisions about American involvement. As before, the perceived economic, strategic, political, and humanitarian interests of the nation will continue to guide policymakers.

When President Jimmy Carter took office in 1977, the United States was not very far removed from the costly and divisive Vietnam War. The mood of the nation, and of Congress, was certainly one of caution regarding foreign intervention. Carter came to the presidency with no background in foreign affairs, but he did have principles. He made human rights the cornerstone of his diplomacy. President Carter had some foreign policy successes, but those gains were overwhelmed by the Iranian hostage crisis and the Soviet invasion of Afghanistan. The Iranian situation, we can now see, was rooted in American support for the Shah. The United States had supported the Shah, like other noncommunist dictators, even though he was anything but democratic. When he was finally overthrown, the United States became an easy target for the new revolutionary power structure. When protesting Iranians overran the American embassy and took American hostages captive in November 1979, President Carter and the United States seemed powerless. Frustration with Carter grew, as the days of Americans held hostage dragged on through the next year. Carter's opponent in the 1980 election, Ronald Reagan, assured the voters that no nation would dare take hostages if he were president.

The Soviet invasion of Afghanistan in the winter of 1979-1980 further complicated President Carter's foreign policies and caused him even more grief at home. To many, the Soviet Union's bold aggression further illustrated American weakness since Vietnam. Actually, President Carter took fairly strong measures to express the disapproval of the United States over Soviet action. Some of those measures, such as canceling a wheat sale and boycotting the 1980 Olympics in Moscow, were unpopular at home. In any event, it would take ten years of resistance by the Afghans and a change in Soviet leadership to convince the Soviets to leave.

The foreign policy problems in Iran and Afghanistan were not the only reasons why President Carter lost the presidential election of 1980. High interest and inflation rates were probably even more important. In hindsight, it is not too hard to understand why the majority of voters rejected Carter, particularly when Ronald Reagan was promising to restore prosperity at home and American power and prestige abroad.

President Reagan began his term in office by intensifying the Cold War rhetoric and vastly accelerating military spending. He claimed that the Soviets were "prepared to commit any crime, to lie, to cheat," and he characterized the Soviet Union as the "focus of evil in the modern world." "Star Wars" seemed more than an imaginative movie scenario, as Reagan pledged that the United States would move ahead with laser-beam technology tied to a Strategic Defense Initiative (SDI).

While the Pentagon went on a spending spree, accompanied by examples of gross excess and corruption, and the Cold War intensified, the Reagan administration seemed to stumble through trouble spots in South Africa, the Middle East, and Central America. Some of the activities in the latter two areas became linked in the infamous Iran-*contra* affair, first exposed in 1986-1987. The revelations showed that administration officials, most notably Oliver North of the National Security Council and William Casey of the Central Intelligence Agency, had been secretly selling weapons to Iran. Apparently they thought that as a nation branded as terrorist by the United States, Iran could use its influence to free

American hostages held by terrorist groups in Lebanon. President Reagan had pledged never to pay ransom for hostages, yet that appeared to be what was transpiring. Furthermore, the profits from the sales of the arms were to be diverted, illegally, to aid the *contras* in Nicaragua.

The whole episode not only brought up questions about the wisdom of American policy, but also it provoked concerns about the competence of President Reagan and of constitutional rule. The threat to the Constitution involved more than the duplicity of selling weapons to terrorists. Casey, North, and the others involved apparently believed that they had the right to circumvent congressional legislation temporarily halting the shipment of United States funds to the *contra* rebels in Nicaragua. Furthermore, when the story of this unseemly affair began to be exposed in late 1986, the major operatives had already begun a cover-up operation that proved to be similar to the Watergate affair of the Nixon era. The public's reaction to Oliver North was especially interesting, for a man who admitted to lies and illegal acts became a national hero to some. He played the media for all it was worth, and he wrapped himself in the flag. Or, as one commentator put it, he tried to destroy the Constitution and hide behind the flag.

Remarkably, while the Iran-*contra* affair was unraveling, American relations with the Soviet Union did an about-face. Why? Some believe that President Reagan's open and friendly demeanor, particularly in reference to new Soviet leadership, was a key. Others cite the massive American military buildup as a major factor in forcing the Soviets to reassess their priorities. The most obvious answer lies not so much in what the United States did in the short term as it does in the emergence of new Soviet leadership. As we now know, former Soviet President Mikhail Gorbachev's bold initiatives dramatically changed the course of world history as well as his own nation.

Soon after Reagan turned over the presidency to George Bush, the Cold War, which had dominated so much of American foreign policy since the 1940s, ended. Gorbachev's decisions to allow eastern European nations to form their own governments and to pursue their own national interests signaled the beginning of a new era in world diplomacy. The collapse of the Soviet Union itself in late 1991 confirmed the end of the old.

The Bush administration faced the challenge of providing direction in this "post-Cold War" world. Initially, it appeared in some ways that things had not changed too much. The United States used its "big stick" in an invasion of Panama in late 1989 to oust strongman Manuel Noriega. Then, when peace seemed to be breaking out all over, the United States led a successful coalition in removing Iraq's invading forces from its neighboring nation of Kuwait. The coalition's easy victory in Operation Desert Storm have led some to conclude that international order will be maintained in a like manner in the future.

As the world enters a new century, it appears that military competition will be less and less important in the relations of the great powers. Issues involving the global environment, world trade, and north-south economic relationships will demand more international attention. The quality of the leadership of the United States in seeking resolution of these and other issues will continue to depend on a clear understanding of our diplomatic history as well as reasoned judgments about future directions.

LEARNING OBJECTIVES

Goal—The purpose of this lesson is to increase our understanding of American foreign policy since 1976.

Objectives—Upon completing this lesson, you should be able to:
1. Evaluate the successes and the limitations of President Jimmy Carter's foreign policy.
2. Analyze President Ronald Reagan's foreign policy.
3. Analyze the factors which led to the end of the Cold War.
4. Examine the American response to the Persian Gulf War of 1990-1991.
5. Assess the diplomatic role of the United States in the post-Cold War world.

TEXT FOCUS POINT

The following questions are designed to help you get the most from your reading. Review them before you do your reading. After completing the assignment, write responses and/or notes to reinforce what you have learned.

Text: Nash et al., *The American People*, Chapter 30, pp. 1014-1026.

1. Describe and explain the successes as well as the failures and limitations of the foreign policy decisions made during the Reagan, Bush, and Clinton administrations.

VIDEO FOCUS POINTS

The following questions are designed to help you get the most from the video segment of this lesson. Review them before you watch the video. After viewing the video segment, write responses and/or notes to reinforce what you have learned.

Video: "The Cold War Ends"

1. What factors shaped President Carter's foreign policy? Why was the human rights policy selectively enforced? How does Professor Joseph Nye assess Carter's handling of crises in Iran and Afghanistan and his other foreign policy decisions?
2. Why did President Reagan change the emphasis of American foreign policy? What problems were associated with the military spending of the 1980s?
3. What factors contributed to the development of the Iran-*contra* affair? In what way did the affair threaten the constitutional balance of power?
4. What explains the changes which took place in the Soviet Union and eastern Europe in the late 1980s?
5. Why did the United States intervene in the Persian Gulf area in 1990-1991? Why did the public respond so favorably to Operation Desert Storm?
6. What will likely characterize the post-Cold War world?

ENRICHMENT IDEA

This activity is not required unless your instructor assigns it. It is offered as a suggestion to help you learn more about the material presented in this lesson.

1. During 1990-1991, the world experienced remarkable changes with the end of the Cold War and the collapse of the Soviet Union. In a well-reasoned 750-word essay, express your understanding of why these events took place and your opinion about what the changes meant for the United States as well as you personally.
2. Read the "Technology Changes the American People" segment about the Internet and the World Wide Web on pages 1016-1017 of your textbook. Write a 750-word essay discussing the questions at the end of the textbook.

SUGGESTED READINGS

See the "Recommended Reading" listings on pages 1024-1025 of the text if you wish to explore further the material presented in this lesson.

SUGGESTED WEB SITES

Several places in the textbook will include information marked "The History Place." This is a reference to a related web site. See the "Suggested Web Sites" at the end of the chapter of the textbook if you wish to further explore the material presented in this lesson.

PRACTICE TEST

The following items will help you evaluate your understanding of this lesson. Use the answer key at the end of the lesson to check your answers or to locate material related in each question.

MULTIPLE-CHOICE INSTRUCTIONS

Choose the single best answer. If more than one answer is required, it will be so indicated.

1. President Ronald Reagan's foreign policy during his first term can best be described as an attempt to
   A. appear aggressive.
   B. remain cautious.
   C. revive détente.
   D. conciliate communists.

2. All of the following factors contributed to the Iran-*contra* affair EXCEPT
   A. congressional caution regarding aid to Nicaragua.
   B. administration officials with little regard for Congress.
   C. respect for constitutional restraints on presidential authority.
   D. desire to free hostages even if it meant dealing with terrorists.

3. The changes which took place in the Soviet Union in the late 1980s and early 1990s were primarily attributable to
    A. clever diplomacy of Ronald Reagan.
    B. reform proposals initiated by Mikhail Gorbachev.
    C. American threats of "Star Wars."
    D. Russian fears of attacks from NATO forces.

4. In the video program, Professor Joseph Nye stated that a mistake made by President Carter during the Iranian hostage crisis was to
    A. negotiate with the Iranian militants.
    B. attempt to rescue the hostages.
    C. become too personally involved.
    D. seek Soviet help in releasing captives.

5. When Ronald Reagan became president, he believed that
    A. Soviet power was rising relative to American.
    B. communism was on the verge of collapse.
    C. global warming was a priority issue.
    D. nuclear disarmament was attainable within five years.

6. The American public responded favorably to the Persian Gulf War for all of the following reasons EXCEPT
    A. issue of good versus evil was expressed.
    B. reassertion of American military capacity was desired.
    C. broad coalition of U.N. support was present.
    D. fear of Soviet control of the region was real.

7. In the video program, Professor Joseph Nye stated his opinion that the post-Cold War world will necessitate
    A. increased military spending by Western powers.
    B. protective trade legislation by the United States.
    C. more complicated analysis of international problems.
    D. removal of national boundaries in Europe.

ESSAY/PROBLEM QUESTION

8. Describe and explain the major developments in American foreign policy between 1977 and the mid-1990s. What did these developments portend for the United States and the world?

ANSWER KEY

Answers	Learning Objectives	Focus Points	References
1. A	2	T1	Nash, p. 1014
2. C	2	T1, V3	Nash, p. 1021 and Video
3. B	3	T1, V4	Nash, pp. 1014-1015 and Video
4. C	1	V1	Video
5. A	2	V2	Video
6. D	4	V5	Video
7. C	4	V6	Video
8.	All	All	Text and Video

Lesson 26

Looking Backward, Looking Forward

LESSON ASSIGNMENTS

Review the following assignments in order to schedule your time appropriately. Pay careful attention; the titles and numbers of the textbook chapter, the telecourse guide lesson, and the video program may be different from one another.

Reader: *Perspectives on America, Volume 2*
"Can We All Get Along?," by Dale Maharidge.

Video: "Looking Backward, Looking Forward,"
from the series *America in Perspective*

OVERVIEW

History teaches everything, even the future.
—Alphonse de Lamartine

The citation above reminds us of how broad our study of the American past has been in this course and suggests that our history will shape our future. In the previous twenty-five lessons, we have traced the development of the United States from a rural to an urban nation, from a minor role player on the world stage to the major actor. In between, we have examined change and continuity in our economic, social, and political history. We have analyzed why change occurs and what limits it. As we go forward, let us continue to use the perspective we have gained from the past to guide our decisions in the present and future.

The lessons of history cannot be applied with exactitude to the future because of different people, pressures, and situations which lie ahead. Yet an understanding of the main currents of our historical experience can help us deal wisely with present and future challenges. As Ernest R. May wrote in *'Lessons' of the Past*, students of history "may develop some skill at least in identifying questions to be asked by those

---

who look ahead." Finally, consider this passage from Robert Heilbroner's book, *The Future as History*:

> We cannot help living in history. We can only fail to be aware of it. If we are to meet, endure, and transcend the trials and defeats of the future, for trials and defeats there are certain to be, it can only be from a point of view which, seeing the future as part of the sweep of history, enables us to establish our place in that immense procession in which is incorporated whatever hope humankind may have. (*The Future as History*, New York: Harper & Row, 1960, p. 209.)

LEARNING OBJECTIVES

Goal—The purpose of this lesson is to encourage reflection upon the major developments in American history since 1877 and to consider how our historical experience shapes our future.

Objectives—Upon completing this lesson, you should be able to:
1. Assess what the study of history can teach us about the past, present, and future.
2. Place in perspective the major economic, political, diplomatic, and social developments in the United States since 1877.
3. Apply the analytical framework developed in this course to your understanding of present and future issues.

READER FOCUS POINTS

The following questions are designed to help you get the most from your reading. Review them before you do your reading. After completing the assignment, write responses and/or notes to reinforce what you have learned.

Reader: *Perspectives on America, Volume 2*, "Can We All Get Along?," by Maharidge.

1. Why was the United States fragmenting culturally in the 1990s? How does the author define American separatists?

2. How do the lives of Michael Dunn, Martha Escutia, Donald Northcross, and Maria Ha reflect the opportunities and challenges of contemporary multicultural American society?

VIDEO FOCUS POINTS

The following questions are designed to help you get the most from the video segment of this lesson. Review them before you watch the video. After viewing the video segment, write responses and/or notes to reinforce what you have learned.

Video: "Looking Backward, Looking Forward"

1. In general, what can history teach us?
2. How far have the American people moved toward equality?   What limits equality?
3. When does creative political change occur?   What is needed beyond politics to bring about change?
4. Why is the United States likely to remain a dominant force in world affairs?
5. What does environmental history teach us?

SUGGESTED READINGS

The following books are recommended to you if you wish to explore further some of the material presented in this lesson:

The Disuniting of America, by Arthur Schlesinger, Jr.
The Future of the Past, by C. Vann Woodward
An Inquiry into the Human Prospect, by Robert Heilbroner
The Lessons of History, by Michael Howard
'Lessons' of the Past, by Ernest R. May

SUGGESTED WEB SITES

Several places in the textbook will include information marked "The History Place." This is a reference to a related web site. See the "Suggested Web Sites" at the end of the chapter of the textbook if you wish to further explore the material presented in this lesson.

PRACTICE TEST

The following items will help you evaluate your understanding of this lesson. Use the answer key at the end of the lesson to check your answers or to locate material related in each question.

MULTIPLE-CHOICE INSTRUCTIONS

Choose the single best answer. If more than one answer is required, it will be so indicated.

1. All of the following can be defined as separatists EXCEPT the
   A. working poor, jobless, and homeless.
   B. wealthy living behind literal and/or symbolic walls.
   C. author of *The Disuniting of America.*
   D. practitioners of "politically correct" ideas.

2. The life of Maria Ha represented
   A. refugees who fled Southeast Asia.
   B. personal achievements earned through hard work and academic excellence.
   C. students experiencing the effects of cultural factionalism.
   D. all of the above.

3. According to historians, it is important to see history as providing
   A. evidence that conflict leads to progress.
   B. proof that conspiracy theories are usually true.
   C. true analogies with present situations.
   D. continuity by which to measure actions and decisions.

4. One of the restraints limiting equality in America in the 1990s is
    A. institutional racism.
    B. lack of voting rights.
    C. legal discrimination.
    D. denial of educational opportunities.

5. In addition to legislation, bringing about positive change in America requires
    A. education of the populace.
    B. violence toward the establishment.
    C. threats to national security.
    D. economic equality for all.

6. In the video program, Professor Joseph Nye suggested that the United States will continue to lead the post-Cold War world for all of the following reasons EXCEPT
    A. cultural and ideological appeal of America.
    B. economic strength of the nation.
    C. undeniable commitment to use its strengths.
    D. military power second to none.

ESSAY/PROBLEM QUESTIONS

7. Describe and explain how and why industry, agriculture, and labor have changed since 1877. What challenges face these sectors of the American economy today?

8. Describe and explain the major cycles of American politics since 1877. What are the major challenges facing political leaders and the political system today?

9. Describe and explain how and why the role of the United States in world affairs changed during the past century. What challenges in world affairs will the United States likely face during the 1990s?

10. Describe and explain how and why the status of minorities (racial, ethnic, women) in America has changed since 1877. What challenges remain for minorities today?

11. Both urbanization and immigration have been major forces in shaping modern America. How and why did America become an urban nation? Why was the United States a nation of immigrants? How has the nation dealt with controlling and assimilating immigrants? What challenges does the United States face today in respect to urban life and immigration policy?

12. Describe and explain the development of the welfare system in the United States during the past century. Explain legitimate criticism of the current welfare system. How could the current system be improved?

13. Describe and explain the development of the conservation/environmental movement over the last century. What explains the successes and failures of this movement? What problems need to be dealt with in this area today?

ANSWER KEY

Answers	Learning Objectives	Focus Points	References
1. C	2	R1	Reader
2. D	2	R2	Reader
3. D	1	V1	Video
4. A	3	V2	Video
5. A	2	V3	Video
6. C	2	V4	Video
7. Comprehensive of all lessons		All	Reader and Video
8. Comprehensive of all lessons		All	Reader and Video
9. Comprehensive of all lessons		All	Reader and Video
10. Comprehensive of all lessons		All	Reader and Video
11. Comprehensive of all lessons		All	Reader and Video
12. Comprehensive of all lessons		All	Reader and Video
13. Comprehensive of all lessons		All	Reader and Video

Contributors

We gratefully acknowledge the valuable contributions to this course from the following individuals. The titles were accurate when the video programs were recorded, but may have changed since the original taping.

LESSON 1—"THE CLOSING OF THE FRONTIER"

Gary Anderson, Professor of History, University of Oklahoma
Julie Roy Jeffrey, Professor of History, Goucher College

LESSON 2—"THE RISE OF BIG BUSINESS"

R. Hal Williams, Professor of History, Southern Methodist University

LESSON 3—"LABOR'S STRUGGLE"

Melvyn Dubofsky, Professor of History, State University of New York—Binghamton
Alice Kessler-Harris, Professor of History and Director of Women's Studies, Rutgers University

LESSON 4—"THE HUDDLED MASSES"

Leonard Dinnerstein, Professor of History, University of Arizona
Zane Miller, Professor of History, University of Cincinnati

LESSON 5—"THE AMERICAN DREAM DEFERRED"

Darlene Clark Hine, John A. Hannah Professor of History, Michigan State University

---

LESSON 6—"THE POPULIST CHALLENGE"

Peter Frederick, Professor of History, Wabash College
Lawrence Goodwyn, Professor of History, Duke University

LESSON 7—"WAR AND EMPIRE"

Robert Beisner, Professor of History, The American University
Lewis Gould, Eugene C. Barker Centennial Professor in American History, University of Texas—Austin
Lester Langley, History Research Professor, University of Georgia

LESSON 8—"THE PROGRESSIVE IMPULSE"

Allen F. Davis, Professor of History, Temple University
Willard Gatewood, Alumni Distinguished Professor of History, University of Arkansas—Fayetteville
Jack Temple Kirby, W. E. Smith Professor of History, Miami University (Ohio)

LESSON 9—"THE PROGRESSIVE PRESIDENTS"

Allen F. Davis, Professor of History, Temple University
Willard Gatewood, Alumni Distinguished Professor of History, University of Arkansas—Fayetteville
Jack Temple Kirby, W. E. Smith Professor of History, Miami University (Ohio)

LESSON 10—"THE BIG STICK"

Robert Beisner, Professor of History, The American University
Lewis Gould, Eugene C. Barker Centennial Professor in American History, University of Texas—Austin
Lester Langley, History Research Professor, University of Georgia

LESSON 11—"THE GREAT WAR"

Otis Graham, Professor of History, University of California—Santa Barbara
David Kennedy, Chair, Department of History, Stanford University

LESSON 12—"TRANSITIONS AND TENSIONS: THE 1920S"

Willard Gatewood, Alumni Distinguished Professor of History, University of
  Arkansas—Fayetteville
Roderick Nash, Professor of History and Environmental Studies, University of
  California—Santa Barbara

LESSON 13—"HARD TIMES: THE GREAT DEPRESSION"

Paul Conkin, Distinguished Professor of History, Vanderbilt University
Robert Heilbroner, Professor of Economics, Emeritus, New School for Social
  Research
Joan Hoff, Professor of History, Indiana University
Studs Terkel, Author and Oral Historian

LESSON 14—"THE NEW DEAL"

Paul Conkin, Distinguished Professor of History, Vanderbilt University
Arthur Schlesinger, Jr., Writer and Historian

LESSON 15—"THE ROAD TO WAR"

Calvin Christman, Professor of History, Cedar Valley College and Univeristy of
  North Texas
Roger Daniels, Professor of History, University of Cincinnati
Robert Divine, George W. Littlefield Professor in American History, University of
  Texas—Austin
Allan Winkler, Chair, Department of History, Miami Univeristy (Ohio)

Contributors

LESSON 16—"THE GOOD WAR"

Stephen Ambrose, Professor of History, University of New Orleans
Calvin Christman, Professor of History, Cedar Valley College and University of North Texas
Robert Divine, George W. Littlefield Professor in American History, University of Texas—Austin

LESSON 17—"THE COLD WAR BEGINS"

Robert Divine, George W. Littlefield Professor in American History, University of Texas—Austin
Richard Fried, Professor of History, University of Illinois—Chicago

LESSON 18—"AN AGE OF CONFORMITY"

Kenneth Hamilton, Professor of History and Director, African-American Studies, Southern Methodist University
William O'Neill, Professor of History, Rutgers University

LESSON 19—"TOWARD THE AMERICAN DREAM"

Julian Bond, Adjunct Professor, The American University
Hugh Davis Graham, Holland N. McTyeire Professor of History, Vanderbilt University
Darlene Clark Hine, John A. Hannah Professor of History, Michigan State University

LESSON 20—"EXPANDING THE AMERICAN DREAM"

Charles Banner-Haley, Professor of History, Colgate University
Julian Bond, Adjunct Professor, The American University
Albert Camarillo, Professor of History, Stanford University
Hugh Davis Graham, Holland N. McTyeire Professor of History, Vanderbilt University
Darlene Clark Hine, John A. Hannah Professor of History, Michigan State University
Alice Kessler-Harris, Professor of History and Director of Women's Studies, Rutgers University
Ricardo Romo, Professor of History, University of Texas—Austin

LESSON 21—"THE LIMITS OF POWER: VIETNAM"

Robert Divine, George W. Littlefield Professor in American History, University of Texas—Austin
George Herring, Professor of History, University of Kentucky

LESSON 22—"THE LIMITS OF POLITICS"

Stephen Ambrose, Professor of History, University of New Orleans
Joan Hoff, Professor of History, Indiana University
Arthur Schlesinger, Jr., Writer and Historian

LESSON 23—"THE CONSERVATIVE RESURGENCE"

Tim Blessing, Professor of History, Pennsylvania State University—Berks Campus
Albert Camarillo, Professor of History, Stanford University
Allan Winkler, Chair, Department of History, Miami University (Ohio)

LESSON 24—"AN ERA OF EXCESS"

Robert Heilbroner, Professor of Economics, Emeritus, New School for Social Research
William O'Neill, Professor of History, Rutgers University
Allan Winkler, Chair, Department of History, Miami University (Ohio)

LESSON 25—"THE COLD WAR ENDS"

Joseph Nye, Jr., Director, Center for International Affairs, Harvard University
John Stoessinger, Distinguished Professor of International Affairs, Trinity University

LESSON 26—"LOOKING BACKWARD, LOOKING FORWARD"

David Kennedy, Chair, Department of History, Stanford University
Otis Graham, Professor of History, University of California—Santa Barbara
Joan Hoff, Professor of History, Indiana University
Kenneth Hamilton, Professor of History and Director, African-American Studies, Southern Methodist University
Albert Camarillo, Professor of History, Stanford University
Darlene Clark Hine, John A. Hannah Professor of History, Michigan State University
Arthur Schlesinger, Jr., Writer and Historian
Stephen Ambrose, Professor of History, University of New Orleans

ISBN-13: 978-1-7290-3084-4

Different Is The Same

Illustrated By: Steve Kalar

Dedication

Our book is dedicated to our children. If we as a nation are to return to the family values that made our nation great, it will be achieved not by politicians, not through legislation, not through more laws, it will be achieved through embedding in our children that respect is one of the most important principles they can possess.

Respect for others, respect for our nation, respect for our environment, respect for their faith, and importantly, respect for themselves. "Different is the Same" is a tool to teach respect and responsibility to our children at an early age. Our children's capacity to learn in their earliest years will set the foundation for the way they live the rest of their lives.

Lastly, this book is also dedicated to our nation's parents. For they are the stewards who have the responsibility to teach their children well. Through our book, we afford parents a chance to chart the direction of their children's future.

Our children are our future, teach them properly and we will do ourselves, our nation, and our world a huge favor. We hope you enjoy "Different is the Same".

The World Can Be Cold And Cruel Isn't It A Shame?

When You
Walk
In Another
Kid's Shoes
We Learn
That

DiFFerent IS The Same

Are Your Ears Too Big,
Your Body Too Large,
Or Your Nose
A Bit Too
Small?

YOU MIGHT POSSESS A DISABILITY THAT CAUSES YOU TO FALL.

Maybe
Your Eyes
Are Too Weak
And
You Need
Glasses To
Clearly See

Or
You Have A
Bad Illness,
It Could
Happen
To
You And Me.

Each Of Us Have Our Insecurities, God Just Made Us All That Way

ANY ONE OF US CAN FACE FAILURE ON ANY GIVEN DAY.

I Remember
AS A
YOUNG BOY
Teasing
Other Kids
AT SCHOOL,

And I Know
It Was Humiliating
For Those I
Taunted
Even Though
I Thought
It Was Cool.

A Wise Person
Taught Me
Something Valuable,
It At Once
Filled
Me With Shame.

Look
At The World
Through The
Other
Person's Eyes
You Will Find
That

DIFFerent
IS The Same.

You See
The Person
With
Those Funny
Ears,
Is Very Gifted
At Math

And The Kid
With A.D.H.D.
Can Go
Very Fast
DoWn
The
RUNNiNG Path.

The Child
Who Is Autistic
Can
Play A Piano
Concerto,
She Is A
Prodigy.

The Boy
In The
Wheel Chair
Can Write
Amazing Stories
That Fascinate
You And Me.

AS We Walk
Through
Each
Moment In Life,
Do Not Live
In
Shame.

Rather Take Joy
In The Fact
That We Now
Know That

DiFFerent IS
The Same

Don't Be
Surprised
When You
Treat
Each Person
With
Dignity And Respect,

That Your Life
Will Become
So Much Better
Because
On So Many Others,
You Have A Most
Positive Affect.

RESPECT YOURSELF AND OTHERS EVERYDAY

EACH OF US IS DIFFERENT IN OUR OWN WAY

STAND UP FOR ONE ANOTHER

PLEDGE EVERY DAY, TO APPRECIATE EACH OTHER

EVEN WHEN WE FEEL LOW

COUNT ON THE KINDNESS AND CONFIDENTLY KNOW

THAT DIFFERENT IS THE SAME!

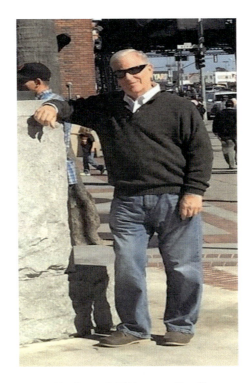

Michael Kincade Sr.

Author

Writing a book is a complicated venture. It takes many pieces to complete the puzzle of a good story. I have been blessed by a number of exceptional pieces that allowed the making of this book. First, my son Brian made an introduction that would be life changing for me. Through his business contacts he introduced us to Mr. Steve Kalar. A world class artist/aesthetics designer, Steve put his remarkable skills to use to illustrate our book. More than illustrate, Steve devoted many hours of his valuable time to not only illustrate, but also design our layout, use the appropriate colors, and create unforgettable characters to enhance our book. Beyond his talent, he is a most giving person. In this process we discovered my daughter-in-law Jennifer possessed innate talents that complimented Steve's work. She not only possesses ubiquitous computer and design skills, but she and Steve, whom I now realize are geniuses each in their own way, communicated on a level that was amazing. Their efforts resulted in a work of art that exceed my most ambitious expectation. To my wife Nancy, thank you for applying your discerning eye to our work and making suggestions that made "Different is the Same" the book it has become. To my son, Matt and daughter-in-law, Tova, thanks for your continued encouragement and support. Finally, to our grandson Gunner, whose presence provided me the inspiration to write this book in the hopes I can do my part to enrich his future and that of all our world's children, who in turn will continue to share this legacy with future generations.

STEVE KALAR
Artist/Aesthetics Designer

I was born in Paso Robles and started selling my paintings at 11 years old while attending the Lillian Larson Elementary School in San Miguel. I graduated from Paso Robles High School, Class of 1970 and began my Fine Arts degree that fall at Stanislaus University in Turlock, California. In the 1980's, I became the only artist to become a member of the Academic Hall of Fame of the Paso Robles High School.

My adventure in Italy began in August of 1972. My parents, Bob & Fern Kalar, offered me the opportunity to study my third year of university with the California International Program in Firenze, Italia. I attended the Accademia Di Belle Arti Di Firenze and studied fine arts studio painting, fresco, and restoration techniques. An emphasis of my artistic journey in Firenze was to paint daily life in the central market of Borgo San Lorenzo over four decades of both living and traveling in Italy. I still remember the first morning I ventured into the market-its beauty of space, seasonal color, and daily life have inspired and overwhelmed me in the past 45 years. Over time my paintings have become a historical collection of the ebb and flow of generations of Florentines living and working in the open market. In 1999, I was asked to become a member of a five hundred year old renaissance colony of artists, "La Societa delle Belle Arti Circolo degli Artisti." (The Society of the House of Dante). In May 2001, I enjoyed my first museum opening of my work at the museum of the House of Dante and the beginning of my dream to return to Europe to Exhibit my art. For 53 years I have been working and continue to work as an artist/aesthetic designer throughout the United States, mainly on the Central Coast of California, creating ambiance, special effects and commissioned art work for a multitude of high-end projects for various clientele.

VISIT THE ARTIST
WWW.STEVEKALAR.COM

What Makes You Different?

_____

_____

_____

_____

You Can Share With Us What Makes You Different And Special At:

"DifferentistheSame.coM"

Made in the USA
Las Vegas, NV
26 October 2021